The Teaching
of Writing
in Our Schools

Richard Corbin

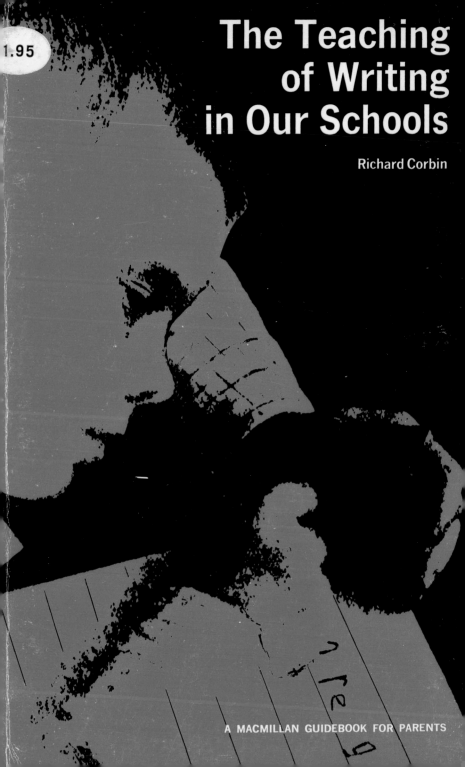

A MACMILLAN GUIDEBOOK FOR PARENTS

2

THE TEACHING
OF WRITING
IN OUR SCHOOLS

A Macmillan Guidebook

for Parents

Richard Corbin

SPONSORED BY THE
NATIONAL COUNCIL OF TEACHERS OF ENGLISH

THE TEACHING
OF WRITING
IN OUR SCHOOLS

The Macmillan Company NEW YORK
Collier-Macmillan Limited LONDON

First Printing

Library of Congress catalog card number: 66–14200

THE MACMILLAN COMPANY, NEW YORK
COLLIER-MACMILLAN CANADA, LTD., TORONTO, ONTARIO

Printed in the United States of America

FOREWORD

Forces are at work to revolutionize the teaching of English: a swelling body of scholarly and pedagogical research, the new demands of a complex society, a heightened professional spirit among teachers. But if revolution is a fact in the teaching of English, so too is conservation. Changes are rarely as dramatic as enthusiastic proponents claim, or as sweeping as opponents insist. Even an overnight curriculum financed through a crash program and instituted by a task force has roots in decades of research, of insight, of vision.

The National Council of Teachers of English is grateful for the opportunity to bring to publication three companion volumes: *The Teaching of Reading in Our Schools* by Ruth Reeves, *The Teaching of Language in Our Schools* by Miriam B. Goldstein, *The Teaching of Writing in Our Schools* by Richard Corbin. It is particularly grateful to the three authors, members of the Council and leaders of their profession, who show not only a grasp of the changing present, but an understanding commitment to the tradition and history that have led to it.

No other subject in the school curriculum commands more attention than English. In secondary schools most students give a minimum of five years to it. In elementary schools the content and the skills of English receive up to 60 per cent of the instructional time and effort. That this discussion of English required three books attests to the scope of English, but not to any natural separations in the subject. As the authors make clear, reading, composition, and language study are inextricably bound together; and the study of literature pervades all three. The National Council of Teachers of English is pleased to commend all three books to parents interested in English programs designed for their children, and to others who seek a clear and accurate picture of the present and the foreseeable future in the teaching of English.

Robert F. Hogan
ASSOCIATE EXECUTIVE SECRETARY
NATIONAL COUNCIL OF TEACHERS OF ENGLISH

v

PREFACE

Is writing important to your child?

In his notable report on the American high school, James Conant recommends that in English classes 50 per cent of the time be given to the teaching of composition.

The National Association of Secondary-School Principals in one of its bulletins emphasizes that "during each school semester, provision must be made to teach writing systematically, sequentially, and continuously."

The Commission on English of the College Entrance Examination Board has stated: "Composition should be neither infrequent nor incidental. It should be part of each week's work and should be intimately connected with other parts of that work."

Even if you as a parent have no strong personal feelings in the matter, these recommendations would seem to be overwhelming evidence that writing *is* important. But most parents do not have to be told this fact. From their own experiences in school, business, or professional life, they know well enough the advantage of being able to put down their thoughts in clear and lively English. Thus, it is entirely understandable that many parents ask themselves uneasily, "What can I do to help my child achieve the skill he should have in writing?" Or that some parents, disturbed at the examples they themselves see or at the school's report on their children's writing, are undecided whether to ask, "What is wrong with my child?" or "What is wrong with the school?"

This book does not pretend to give "nice" answers to these difficult questions. What it does attempt is to acquaint you, as an interested parent, with the nature of the writing act, with the methods used generally in schools to develop your child's writing ability, and finally to suggest some practical ways in which you as a parent can help both your child and the school in their common endeavor.

Richard Corbin

CONTENTS

WHY TEACH WRITING?

1

As a parent you are bound to come, sooner or later, face to face with your child's first out-of-the-classroom writing assignment, called technically the "composition." This event may occur as late as the time he or she enters seventh grade, though it varies from one school to another; schools and even teachers within a school employ different time tables and procedures for teaching written composition. As early as the late primary grades, you may have shared your child's experience of planning and writing an "autobiography" with its brief vital statistics and its wide-eyed aspirations to become a television star or an astronaut. You may have been somewhat disturbed at the occasional misspelled word, the amorphous sentence structure, and inadequate paragraphing; but you have realized that the skills of writing are many and that in the school years to come, your child should learn what is still lacking. Many children do, indeed, learn to write a few consecutive paragraphs quite creditably before entering the junior high school. Others, for one reason or another, still misspell, write incomplete or awkwardly constructed sentences, and organize their ideas poorly when writing that "composition" as a home assignment in seventh grade or even beyond.

Writing is not the simplest of human activities. Your child has to travel a long, long road from no writing skills at all, via the experiences of using his teacher as secretary to set down his ideas and later of copying what has been put on the chalkboard or note pad for him, before he is able independently to write meaningful sentences and well-organized paragraphs. In such independent writing, he must meet multiple demands in the way of collecting, selecting, and organizing information, choosing suitable words, employing sentences that are clear to any prospective reader, and, it is hoped, at the same time being reasonably correct in spelling, capitalization, punctuation, and manuscript form.

To illustrate—you probably recall that first notice your six-year-old brought home from school: "First grade has open house Friday at two. Please come. Love, Jimmy." Jimmy had copied in his still

uncertain manuscript writing a real message that he and his classmates had discussed and whose wording they had decided upon under
the teacher's guidance. Jimmy was learning the magic of pencil-on-
paper in conveying ideas to persons not present at the time of writing.
He had written with purpose. Or, recall your pride when first-grader
Vivian brought home her colorful drawing of the many-rayed sun
shining on a flower bed and on it the sentence she had planned and
printed by herself (with some help in spelling): "The sun smells
the flowers." This was Vivian's way of expressing her childish but
nevertheless real delight at the coming of springtime. Nostalgically,
you shared her feeling; yet, at the same time, you saw evidence of
immaturity in her thinking as she ascribed human traits to the inani-
mate sun. Or perhaps it was Mike who, when in third grade, rejected
the imaginative story in his reader and investigated to find the real
reason for the leaves' changing color in the fall. Do you recall how
he sent you to the encyclopedia and your old science textbook to
help him find out the facts? You probably still have his working copy
of the report he wrote at home for posting on the bulletin board:

> In the fall the green leaves turn bright red and yellow. They
> change color because a kind of cork grows between them and the
> stems. Then the sap cannot go into the leaves. So they change
> color. After a while they fall off the tree.

Then you knew that Mike was really learning how to put his ideas
into writing, that years ahead, when he would reach seventh grade,
his first assigned out-of-the-classroom composition would hold few
fears for him—or for you!

Writing is, indeed, the capstone of the communication process.
When your child entered school, he was already a competent if sometimes erratic listener, well able to translate many of the things told
him into action. He could already speak well enough to make most
of his needs known and, on occasion, to exert a considerable influence
upon you, his classmates, or any other people with whom he happened to be associated.

Furthermore, by listening and speaking effectively (and this is
something you may never have thought about before), he was also
demonstrating in a most convincing fashion the fact that he understood the "fundamentals" of English grammar—the basic sentence
patterns and most of the grammatical usages that all English-speaking
people use in passing their thoughts back and forth from one to
another. For this, you as his parents may take a bow, because he

learned these essential matters mainly by imitating you, though you may not have fully realized at the time what was taking place.

If you provided your child with alphabet blocks, picture books, and other simple language materials suitable to his age, it is even possible that your child came to school with an elementary knowledge of reading. Of course, the extent of this reading was probably restricted to the recognition of a few simple words or phrases, like *popsicle, Channel 2,* or *Susie Smith,* but the basic mechanics of the reading act were there—he had learned how to convert written symbols into ideas, whether through your help or his own discovery does not really matter.

The one communication skill your child may know little about when he enters school is writing. Listening, speaking, and even, to some extent, reading are natural acts because they depend on natural tools—the ears, voice, and eyes. But writing requires the use of an artificial tool—a pencil, pen, or typewriter—and an active, rather than a relatively passive, ability to turn symbols into meaning.

Young children, up to the age of six or seven, normally have limited physical ability to control a pencil and have barely started to gain skill in manipulating language symbols for this purpose. In first grade they do learn to use manuscript writing—what you may call printing—because the simple arcs, circles, and perpendicular lines of this type of writing make no great demands on muscular coordination, and children of even nursery school or kindergarten age can quite easily copy the manuscript writing message they want to send someone such as their grandmothers. By the time your child is in third or fourth grade, he probably will have learned to do the cursive form of handwriting that many adults expect of him. Even before this time, he may have acquired the ability to write sentences of his own quite creditably in the simple manuscript writing he had learned to use.

You should keep in mind that your child is "writing" when he dictates to the teacher the sentences he wants put on record. (Perhaps at the same time in his office downtown his father is dictating his ideas to a secretary!) He may do this as an individual and later copy the teacher's transcription of his sentences. Or, he may be one of a group discussing mutual plans for a visit to the zoo or some other common experience and then working out a series of sentences on the subject which the teacher writes on the chalkboard. Usually the children read through such a "composition" under the teacher's guidance to check on its completeness and arrangement. If it is an important plan or story of experiences, the teacher probably copies it on chart paper for future reference. She is making a so-called "reading chart." At any rate, your child is experiencing a necessary initial stage in learning to write down his ideas; at the same time, he is gaining in ability to read.

The Infants Schools in England and certain schools in the United States have been experimenting with a "language-experience" curriculum in which the children learn to write and to read concurrently. How the San Diego County schools encourage children to write as well and as soon as they can is described in a mimeographed report, *Children Write,* by the Publications Committee. Samples of writing by pupils illustrate how writing and reading go hand in hand in this county's language-experience approach to reading. The report states:

> Creative writing can be a classwide experience or it can be the efforts of a small group working at a table with the teacher. Either experience follows a common discussion period where children "think together" and express themselves freely. In the small group method the members work faster and the interest factors and feelings of success are high. The teacher is immediately able to supply needed words or correct spelling, to stimulate thinking and to build curiosity. Another group works with the teacher during the next writing time. During the classwide writing experience children are urged to get their thoughts on paper and not be concerned about spelling, neatness, or correctness. The teacher has placed words and phrases from the preceding discussion on the chalkboard or chart paper and now supplies needed words (as children request help) on small slips of paper or additional chalkboard area, or suggests that the children use published dictionaries or ones they have made as well as other reference resources.
>
> Many preschool children have imaginary playmates and imaginary experiences. To make up stories seems to be a natural occurrence as well as an infectious one and they bring this ability with them when they enter school. Some children have difficulty telling and writing stories because they have not had these previous imaginative experiences. . . .
>
> Children learn many things when they write. They become familiar with proofreading, and with selecting, eliminating and arranging words. However, the first efforts are usually not well done and contain misspelled words, incomplete sentences, and meager punctuation and capitalization. The first stories are not corrected, but as the child reads his story to the teacher, his voice indicates beginnings and endings. He then adds his own periods, question marks, and capitals. . . .[1]

[1] *Children Write,* South Bay Union School District, Imperial Beach, California. Used by permission of the San Diego County Department of Education and South Bay Union School District, Robert Burress, superintendent.

A first-grader wrote the following uncorrected story at the left. The corrected version at the right is a transcription of her oral reading of the story she had just written. Note that the general patterns of the sentences in the two versions are almost identical, but that Gail lacked the technical skill to show the sentences as she said them. She had much yet to learn, but Gail was already well on the road to competency in writing.

The Funny Long Miss Lady	The Funny Long Miss Lady
(as originally written by Gail)	(as read by Gail and transcribed by the teacher)
There was a funny long lady who wanted to be short she ascked all over town wrere she can get to bee short. Then one day she ascked a gril name Lullul then Lullul had to think then she said I no go to the woods and you will fide some wish water.	There was a funny long lady who wanted to be short. She asked all over town how she could get to be short.
	Then one day she asked a girl named Lulu. Lulu had to think, then she said, "I know. Go to the woods and you will find some wish water."
She wet to the wish water and she got her wish. And she shrunk.	She went to the wish water and she got her wish. She shrunk.

WRITING BEGINS WITH TALK

A child begins talking at an early age, generally with the sound *da* or some close approximation, and progresses by the time he enters school to the point where he may make such a sophisticated observation as "Granddaddy has lots of money, hasn't he? Why doesn't Daddy have lots of money?"

Although *da* has no dictionary meaning, parents seem to have no difficulty in recognizing its referent. For a while in their pride and excitement, and especially with the first child or two, they may go ambitiously to work to expand the child's vocabulary: "See the *doggie?* Nice *doggie*. Now say *doggie* for Mommy." The effect upon the adult vocabulary of such forced feeding in infancy is questionable. Fortunately, most parents soon discover that there aren't enough hours in the day to wash the diapers, mix formulas, earn the rent— and also serve as full-time teacher. Parents do not mean to lose interest in their child's linguistic progress, but the earthier demands of life interfere, so that finally the majority of children arrive at their ability to talk intelligibly pretty much on their own.

As the child progresses from the monosyllable *da* to the more sophisticated utterance, such as the one about granddad, it is usually not because he has been taught to say the latter, but because he is growing and gaining greater control of his vocal apparatus and because he has heard certain words often enough that he can manage to imitate their sounds deliberately and meaningfully.

So, in the four or five years that follow the initial experience with *da,* the child literally teaches himself to speak by listening and by associating the sounds he hears with the experiences they accompany. By *imitating* not only the sounds, but the peculiar arrangement of these sounds in the patterns that he hears, and then by relating them to the world around him, your child soon learns to use spoken language with a considerable degree of success.

Learning to express himself in the written language, however, comes about in quite a different and not so easy a way. Though a few children manage on their own, because they have an abnormally strong curiosity or drive, to put down meaningfully some of the graphic symbols that we call writing, it is entirely normal for most children to arrive at school on their first day able to talk fluently—but entirely ignorant of what it means to write. Indeed, the central purpose of the school, though it never neglects to continue developing the child's ability to express himself orally, is to teach him to understand the writings of others and to put his thoughts and feelings into writing of his own.

A child learns to speak in part as naturally as a gibbon learns to gibber or a crow to caw, though with this unique intelligence the child can carry the process far beyond anything achieved by his furred and feathered friends. In contrast, writing is partially an unnatural activity. The manipulation of a pencil or pen is easy enough; but the necessity of dealing with visual symbols in writing calls for skill that is learned with great effort, for the power of abstraction is possessed only by human beings. Only mankind can communicate in writing—and man had to invent the system of symbols that he uses to do it. Witness the fact that gibbons do not write novels, nor do crows write letters to other crows!

DOING WHAT DOES NOT COME NATURALLY

Your child must learn consciously to write. This implies, of course, that he must be deliberately *taught* to write. Imitation, which had such an important role in his learning to speak, plays only a minor part in the process of learning to write. Its main contribution is in the preliminary stage of learning to form the letters of the alphabet, which is handwriting but not communication, though alert children "pick up" a considerable vocabulary and ability to spell from careful observation of their verbal environment.

Like most other acquired skills, learning to put their thoughts down on paper is easier for some children than for others. Sensitivity to words, acute visual memory, unusual powers of observation, strong social or esthetic drives, higher verbal intelligence—it is not clear what combinations of these and other traits in the child determine whether he will grow up to become the next Robert Frost, an unknown illiterate, or like most of us, something in-between—people able to write well enough the letters, reports, and other practical matters that our business and social affairs require, but never entirely comfortable about what we are doing.

Few children learn outside of school to write down their ideas, for the master key to successful learning is normally a trained teacher. Though most of us parents know how to write and like to consider ourselves in some degree teachers, few of us remember very exactly the steps we ourselves went through in learning to write. The trained teacher is not only aware of the steps up which he must lead his pupils; he is also well versed in the methods most likely to succeed. A good part of his advantage lies in the fact that he has observed closely hundreds of children in the process of learning to write as well as to speak their language.

More important than his knowledge of the mechanics of writing is the trained teacher's understanding of the ways to motivate pupils to write. True—most first-graders show spontaneous enthusiasm as they tell their stories and see them magically take shape on the chalkboard or on paper as the teacher writes from dictation. Many of these children continue to take pleasure in expressing their ideas and feelings when the teacher no longer serves as amanuensis, especially if each child is permitted to write information or explanations of things to which he closely relates or is stirred to imaginative storytelling or verse writing. When children write with purpose and at the same time are successfully learning the requisite skills for writing down their increasingly mature, complex ideas, they are likely to write willingly, even eagerly. Enthusiasm for writing fades with the years whenever their writing assignments become impersonal, abstract, and unrelated to their real interests. Only skillful teaching can generate in older disenchanted children pride in their writing and a feeling of personal satisfaction in writing well a report on such remote topics as "The Articles of Confederation" or "The Process of Osmosis."

Children unfortunate enough not to have well-trained teachers of English, with few exceptions, find writing a drudgery. To most it seems an artificial hurdle set between them and the magic word "graduation." By absorption they learn enough about the conventions of writing "to get by." They seldom have their eyes opened to the satisfaction or the even more substantial value that putting down one's thoughts and feelings on paper, exactly and vividly, offers the educated mind.

In our emphasis upon the importance of good teaching, however, we must not forget an easily discernible fact—whatever their advantages, not all people are, or can be, equally good writers. If this were not so, we would all be Shakespeares. Some of us are not good writers because we never made the necessary effort, but others of us are not good writers simply because we lack the ability (though we may have made out very well indeed as technicians or businessmen).

And our children are no different. Some have such a high degree of aptitude for writing that the perceptive teacher can only try to keep out of the way of their progress.

To make clear how our children think and write at various ages and why they do their writing, several actual classroom compositions are quoted verbatim. (The purposes for the writing are in italics.) The first three were written independently by children aged six, who had been taught to read and write the previous year on an experimental basis in an English Infants School. One child wrote in order to *make a record* and used the very short sentences so often used by beginning writers. He wrote:

> In October we had wind for three days. There was hail too. The Roads were flooded. Some trees were blown down. The sea was very rough.

Another six-year-old tried to *spread the news* as she wrote in more fluent style:

> On Saturday I went to Whipsnade Zoo and I saw a baby wolf, it was crippled. Then I went to see the elephant.
> We went to see the flamingoes. They were pink. Then we went to see the bears and it was feeding time, then we went home.

Note her difficulty in punctuating her sentences, which would have caused her no trouble in saying them orally. While she was thinking sequentially, she recounted one detail after another by using "and" to connect somewhat unrelated sentences or by adding a descriptive sentence, as after "wolf" and "flamingoes." (A mature child would likely write: "wolf which was crippled" or "we went to see the pink flamingoes.")

Late in the school year still another pupil in the same class wrote *a report* on information he had gained. He wrote with considerable clarity, selected ideas well, had logical sequence, but still had some trouble in beginning sentences differently and with punctuating the list of animals' names. He wrote:

> The herdsmen lived in this country after the cavemen thousands of years ago. They came over the sea. They caught wild animals and made them tame, cows goats pigs and sheep. They lived on the hills. The grass was good for the animals. They made funny houses with a tree trunk in the middle and branches for a roof. They found out how to make pots from clay and they made tools from flints which they dug out of the ground.

Even poetry, generally considered the most complex form of human expression, is not beyond the reach of young writers, especially if they have had a great many poems read to them at home or by their teachers. From attempts at verse writing a child can learn a great deal about such essentials of good writing as economy, clarity of expression, and the apt use of words.

The following sequence of poems written by first- to sixth-graders in the San Diego, California, City Schools illustrates nicely the progression in thinking, in sentence forms, and in vocabulary that may typically be expected in the elementary grades, though it must be kept in mind that these poems were selected as "the best," which means that most students will not write as well. (The ideas and the words are original with the child; in some instances, the teacher helped in making revisions.)[2]

> Cows are big.
> Cows are fat.
> Cows give milk
> And things like that.
> *Grade 1*

> A tree is big.
> A tree is small.
> A tree is a seed
> That has grown tall.
> *Grade 2*

> When there is fog
> There is nothing but you.
> Nothing but a circle of land
> And you.
> *Grade 3*

[2] *Creative Writing,* San Diego City Schools, San Diego, California. Used by permission of the San Diego City Schools.

The woods are dry, the hills are brown.
The thunder cracks, the rain comes down.
I don't mind that I can't play
Because we need the rain today.

The rain will turn the brown hills green.
The desert flowers, so long unseen,
Will blossom this spring; and in the wood
Tall ferns will wave where nothing stood.

Grade 5

Nature has opened her springtime curtain
    To let us venture inside
To the mountains filled with poppies
    And where the violets hide.

On canyon walls and near mountain streams,
    A mass of colors unfolds.
Sweet lilacs and buttercups close their petals
    On fields with a carpet of gold.

Grade 6

The individuality of the young child shows clearly in his writing, and many of the desirable qualities of the successful adult writer are to be found also in the prose writing of the young, as illustrated in these excerpts from the writing of first- and second-grade children.

Do you think this first-grader may have heard some Kipling stories?

Once upon a time a giraffe had a short neck. One day he happened to swallow a jack from a car. He began to hiccup. Every time he did, his neck got longer and longer. That is why the giraffe has a long neck.

A second-grader may have enjoyed Thurber's *Many Moons* before she wrote:

I looked up at the sky. There was no moon. I looked on the ground and I saw a fairy. He took a gold piece, and with his magic he turned it into a big gold moon.

Comparable to color blindness and tone deafness, a certain number of children (though fortunately not many) have neither a feeling for nor success with written language. Most of these unfortunate children are also handicapped readers. Take, for example, this first page of a nine-page report submitted by a sixteen-year-old, non-academic high school boy on a subject that was dear to his heart. The reader may find it difficult to believe, but not a word or a letter of this sixteen-year-old boy's composition has been altered.

Pigeons

My S.A. is about Pigeons and how They live

Pigeons are a very good hibe they are not expenses and they are very frenly birds, they are all kinds of pigeons but I got only homing birds, I have them because there the most interesting birds of all, there are all name for homming birds to such as grizzel, blue bar, red, black, white, bluecheck, splash, and many other's Homming pigons are good birds they use them in the 1st war and in the 2 war but now they have better ways of doing it.

The way a pigoens makes up with a diffent bird he daces around the remail the mail bird is call the cock and the fremail is called a han. After the cock and hen are meated up they lay eggs 2 of them after they have been sitting on them for two weeks they hacth the baby are a cock and han, when they are first bore they have little yellow hairs, and after two weeks they start to get frathers two weeks more they start walking around there fly inside thar coops by the time there are 2 month's old you take them out for a fly almost 1 mile away then you wate a couple of weeks and take them 5 miles than take them 15, 20, 25, all the way to 500 miles but chances are you will lose about 5 out of 12 and if not more.

Freeding homming pigeons are diffent from ather birds so you get to take better care of them you have to give them fresh water each day and feed them 2 times a day, there food contains of pees hold carn, will I don't know all what they eat but you have to feed them greate have it in a feeder all the time it help thim dejust there food and its good to have cool in the cope small pieces of it keeps them from getting sick.

A reader who bothers to mine below the amazing (but not entirely unreasonable) phonetic spellings and the obviously illiterate solecisms of this composition will detect some nuggets of information about pigeons, and even a kind of eloquence that could grow only out of a deep interest in and knowledge of the writer's subject. Are the school and the teacher to blame for this kind of writing? If the boy had had private tutors every day of his life, it is likely that he would have written no better. His phonetic spellings parallel closely his habitual mispronunciations of the words. His grammatical errors are the same that marked his speech. Yet today the writer of this composition is a respected citizen, a father, a substantial wage earner in his community. Should he have been forced out of school on the basis of his inabilities? Where in his immaturity would he have turned in our demanding society? Today, of course, we would recognize him for what he is—and actually was fifteen years ago—a disadvantaged student. Whether or not this diagnosis at an early age would have helped him attain control of standard written English is a matter of conjecture.

For contrast, read this introduction to an unassigned essay (that is, an "extra" noncredit composition) written by a fourteen-year-old tenth-grade girl in a school for gifted students.

Gallows Humor

Last night the four of us were seated around the dining-table with the dregs and pieces of our supper, and since the food was eaten we began to talk.

Mother is the only one in our family who can tell a good story. Dad insists upon weighting his syllables, upon dropping like rocks into our midst his pear-shaped tones. Danny *will* remain doggedly with one subject, pulling at it, picking it up and bouncing it, until it escapes to a corner to die. And I—oh it's easy to make me talk, but I'm told that what comes out is a melange of French words, my own special versions of Anglo-Saxon originals, which I think show taste and talent, and an unbearable narcissistic chattering.

Mum is the only one who can progress from one point to another, and her voice is pleasant, slightly mid-eastern still, so that the chandelier might possibly be a warm fire, and the whirring of the air conditioner might be a bitter cold wind in Michigan.

"I went to Loehmann's today," she started, "to get a patio dress. I'm so proud of fitting into a size ten now that I thought I deserved it. Really, with the money I saved from not eating—and there were exquisite things there. I tried on some Norman Norell suits, and —you should have seen me. I thought I looked ghastly, like a real *shicksa,* my hair hanging in delightfully nylonlike strands—but I suppose not, some people turned around and looked at me while I was trying on clothes."

I have to explain that Loehmann's is on Fordham Road. It's— I don't know what you could call it, except that the owners buy beautiful clothes for very little, and can afford to sell them for approximately half of what other stores charge. Possibly the store itself isn't splashing fountains and private rooms, but it's utilitarian. It keeps your mind on what you came for.

There can be no argument over the fact that diverse economic, social, and cultural backgrounds account in some degree for the contrasting ability of these two young people to express themselves in writing (or in spoken English, for that matter). Yet no one could reasonably theorize, either, that by exchanging their natural writing abilities, with more advantages, the less proficient boy might have become at least a literate writer; and with fewer, the girl would still have learned to express her thoughts and feelings effectively.

The point of this comparison is not to suggest that some children should and others should not be given the opportunity to learn to the best of their ability. It does suggest that the teacher is faced with the practical problem of apportioning his time and energy fairly among his students according to their needs and abilities—not to mention the needs of our society. The problem in some cases goes beyond even the reach of a Solomon's wisdom. At times, indeed, the school curiously resembles an army in its ability to misgauge and misdirect the human potential.

GETTING THEM TO WRITE

Most children accept writing in the early stages as a new and exciting adventure. They find pleasure in "telling" about their pets, their family life, their day-to-day experiences whether at home or at school. As they grow older and advance in school, the novelty may wear off; but real purpose and strong motivation can and will continue—whenever honest communication of ideas and feelings is involved. If a child has managed to locate information or an explanation that his associates have been seeking, if he has had an unusual experience to tell about, if he has "dreamed up" an intriguing plot or devised some clever verse, he is likely to welcome the opportunity to write and to share what he has written. On the other hand, writing may become a chore if a class is handed a topic on which all are to write in routine fashion or if the teacher is more concerned with technical accuracy than with the idea the writer is trying to convey.

Instead of teachers who are sympathetic audiences for whatever they have to say or write, who always have a kindly and encouraging word for them, these older children find their teachers more and more concerned with restrictive adult concepts such as "correctness" and "pass or fail." In subjects other than English, such as history or science, they are frequently assigned overly long reports to write on topics that have not been made meaningful to them. They are not even sure that these papers are read (many of them, indeed, are not), and in many cases they come to the not always refutable conclusion that the teacher rewards "bulk" rather than "good writing" with higher grades. This conclusion in turn encourages them to resort to textbook parroting and even outright plagiarism.

Some colleges that prepare teachers are already working to solve the problem of their students' deterioration in writing skill after they have completed their college course in freshman English. For instance, Central Connecticut State College in New Britain makes three checks on its students' proficiency in language: (1) at college entrance; (2) at time of admission to the teacher education program; and (3) prior to registration for student teaching. At the University of Kansas and at Duke University, seniors take required examinations to determine their competence in using English; those failing to use standard English well must do remedial work. At least one state has legislation that requires that a prospective teacher be competent in written composition; Title 5 of the California Administrative Code and Education Code specifies that an applicant for the standard teaching credential with a specialization in elementary teaching must demonstrate competency in composition in one of two ways: (1) successfully passing a course in composition, or (2) passing a special examination given by the teacher education institution in lieu of a course in composition.

The teacher of English often finds himself engaged not in teaching his pupils composition, but in removing their deep-seated prejudices against it. He will not achieve this by lectures or by painting falsely rosy pictures of how "easy" writing is. For writing is not easy; it is work, and for most people it is hard work. His best course is to set up discussions and projects so exciting to his students that they accept the writing involved as a natural consequence of their interest. When they begin to recognize that writing can be meaningful and personally satisfying, they are ready to be taught. But remolding students' attitudes toward writing takes more patience and effort than this brief discussion probably suggests. It also requires skillful, well-trained teachers.

This last observation may suggest to perceptive readers that, overshadowing all other factors, how well their children learn to write will depend mainly on the quality and training of the teacher *for whom* they write. And this indeed will be a recurring theme of this book. It isn't news that teachers, like parents and children, are human beings with different interests and varying degrees of ability. By the nature of things, it could not well be otherwise. Some teachers have a special talent for making history come alive, the forte of some is the abstract language of mathematics, and some make science seem the most vital of all subjects. Most of our problems in motivating writing would be solved if all teachers were equally interested in and capable of teaching good composition in the context of their subject fields. But this is a dream. By the time college students preparing for teaching in the various content areas have taken the special courses required of them, few have an opportunity to squeeze into their programs even elementary courses in actual composition or even the teaching of composition. Unfortunately, this is at present a fact of life.

We do have a right to expect, however, that any teacher who is licensed to teach English, either as a minor or a major subject, should be able to interest children in writing and to show them how to write better. Like everyone else, English teachers have their particular interests—some take most of their training in literature, others in speech, still others in composition. Whatever his special concern, each teacher of English has a responsibility not to neglect the teaching of writing. To that end, this book is directed at teachers of English (which include teachers at the elementary and at the secondary level) as well as parents.

But let's keep the problem in perspective. Personal criticism of your child's teacher is more likely to produce a resentful human being than a better teacher. Even good teachers of composition face insuperable odds, which will be discussed in later chapters. Many poorly trained teachers were not so trained of their own choice, as the National Council of Teachers of English pointed out in the 1961 report, *The National Interest and the Teaching of English.* More recently the inadequacies of training and certification scored in this statement have been powerfully underlined by James B. Conant in his comprehensive report, *The Education of American Teachers,* published in 1963.

Only a thoroughgoing romanticist can believe that a "100 per cent perfect" school system is possible. Who among the critics of the American public schools is certain what a 100 per cent perfect school system should be or even what it might do for our children? On the other hand, only an embittered cynic can maintain that our schools cannot be improved. In between these extreme positions are the rest of us, mainly the parents, faced with the realities of our neighborhood school, interested primarily in our John or Mary, but also concerned about the larger problems threatening the nation and the world. In the overall picture of education, good writing is basic but only a part. If it is basic, however, then it demands our attention. Only by common understanding of the complex factors involved and by cooperative thinking and action on the part of parents, school administrators, college teachers, critics, *and* teachers of English, will our schools be able to train our children to write with the skill demanded by our incredibly complicated and constantly changing mode of life.

Should your child be taught to write to the extent that he is able? On what grounds can a parent or a teacher even ask!

OUR TWO LANGUAGES

2

A recent magazine cartoon pictures a Neanderthal couple gazing at each other with expressions that seem to suggest affection mixed with vexation and annoyance. The caption under the cartoon reads: "Now that we've learned to communicate, what are we going to talk about?"

Though we don't and never will know how man discovered language and its uses thousands upon thousands of years ago, we would probably not be far wrong in suspecting some truth beneath the irony in this cartoonist's theory about our ancestors' earliest experiences with language. It seems entirely sensible to assume that, at some stage in his development, man had something to say and an irresistible urge to say it—and that somehow he happened upon a system that worked. It is entirely likely that he communicated with gestures and signals for thousands of years before he discovered the greater efficiency of sounds. It seems also likely that whatever ideas (more likely, feelings) this early man felt compelled to express were completely and utterly simple compared to even the most basic expressions of modern man, even of those who still depend upon their blowguns in Amazonian jungles. For if a parent finds it difficult to empathize with a child a mere twenty years his junior, how could he possibly understand the mental processes of a ten-thousand-year-old ancestor! Still, after all this time, we have never found a better way of communicating with our fellow beings than by talking.

Though the exchange of ideas through the use of sounds is amazingly effective, it has some drawbacks. It works, for example, only if the speaker and the listener are in agreement as to what the sounds stand for. If the speaker uses only sounds that are recognized in Washington and the listener knows only sounds that are understood in Moscow, the communication line—even a "hot line"—is dead. People who speak the same language, however, are as a rule in agreement about most of the sounds used and the ideas they stand for. Thus, at the lunch counter, when you turn to your English-speaking neighbor and make the sounds *Would you pass me the salt, please,* you are rather confident that he will not instead pour catsup on your head.

Because most of us spend our lives among people who "speak our language," we are not often concerned about Russian, French, or Chinese sounds. That is, we are not seemingly affected in our personal affairs. As the world grows smaller, though, and its interests and affairs become more intricately interwoven, we are dutifully, if somewhat less than wholeheartedly, asking our children to master systems of speech sounds other than our own. And we make this concession even when we are not at all satisfied with the progress they are making with their own language, English!

Besides the problem of exchanging ideas with fellow beings who don't know the language, men rather early awoke to another serious flaw in their unique discovery. Communicating with speech sounds worked well enough, but only if the speaker and listener were alive at the same time and within earshot of each other. This problem has been partly solved in our time, of course, by means of such devices as telephone, tape recorder, radio, television, and Telstar. Early men had no such handy instruments to amplify the power of their ears. When they began to feel an urgent need to listen to the dead, to speak to the unborn, or even more practically to talk with their cousins three mountain valleys to the north, human "intelligence" grappled with the problem. After a number of mild but preparatory successes (we are theorizing) with smoke puffs, rock scratchings, and colored stones, man came up with what is undebatably the most ingenious of all human inventions since speech—a *written language*.

Writing not only solved the problem of "talking" at a distance, but it also made possible the storing of ideas. For the first time, men could receive, directly and unedited, suggestions for improving their daily lot from ancestors dead, lo, those many years. Or men who felt a sense of responsibility for the future of their kind could advise their children's children (whom they would never see) how to better conduct their lives. In the long run, as it turned out, this new ability to accumulate and store information and "wisdom" and then to pass it along to future generations (us, that is) has certainly proved the greatest value of all.

We have, in effect, two languages—the spoken and the written. But writing itself apparently began and has since developed in two different ways. In the East, let us use China as our example, writing took the form of drawing the objects referred to—a human figure, a tree, a bird, and so on. At first these pictures were probably entirely literal. But with experience, Chinese writers learned to combine their increasingly conventionalized pictures in order to suggest more complex ideas. For example, by combining pictures of a human being, a skirt, and a broom, they could "write" *housewife*. One cannot read ancient Chinese literature and not be impressed by the ability of the writers to suggest profound and abstract ideas within the limits of a purely pictorial language. The fact that the Chinese have a reputation for being realists, at least in their perception of the sensual world, can, we are told, be traced directly to their language. By forcing the writer to picture "things," the language focused the writer's eye on the physical, sensual world. He could think abstractly, but if he wanted to put his abstract thoughts into writing, he had to find a way to suggest them through pictures.

In the long run, this method has proved to have drawbacks. In a world increasingly concerned with the abstractions of science, the use of picture language has proved inadequate. But this is not all, for in such a system there is no relation at all between the spoken and the written language. Two educated Chinese from different provinces have no trouble communicating in writing. But face to face, they might find it almost impossible to understand each other's speech. If they are uneducated (that is, cannot read or write their language), communication by language in either form is almost impossible. What is true of Chinese is true of any other "picture" language.

A far more efficient system of writing (and fortunately, the ancestor of our own) was worked on in turn by the Egyptians, the Phoenicians, and the Greeks. Unlike the picture languages, it used a system of symbols, or marks, standing for the sounds in the spoken language. This set of symbols became the alphabet used, with variations, by all of the modern languages of the Western world. In English, to take a specific example, we have twenty-six alphabetical symbols that stand for more than forty speech sounds (the letter *a*, for instance, stands for at least four different common sounds, as in h*a*te, h*a*t, p*a*r, and f*a*ther). Putting these letters together into words and then into sentences, we are able to communicate in writing most of our ideas with considerable efficiency.

But no language is perfect. The Chinese student has to spend many years, we are told, to learn enough pictographs to read with understanding even a simple news story. Learning to write Chinese is an even lengthier process. Because the sounds he makes in speech are entirely unrelated to the pictures he draws, the Chinese student has no "phonetic" problems to deal with. In our sense, for example, there is no such thing as a bad Chinese speller. An English student, on the other hand, masters a relatively extensive written vocabulary at an early age, but all of his life he is plagued by our "accidental" system of spelling. (If your child is an incorrigibly poor speller, part of the blame at least can be laid to the fact that in English we do not have letters enough to correspond to all of the speech sounds that we use. Ideally we should have a separate letter for each of the sounds that we use when speaking our language, but in fact we do not.)

A single speech sound by itself, of course, is meaningless. Only when we unite several sounds in combinations that we call *words,* and then combine words in groups or patterns that we call *sentences,* do we produce real meaning. In speaking, the sounds represented by *o, d,* and *g* have no meaning in themselves. Put together as *dog* or *god,* they immediately become symbols for generally recognizable objects or ideas, though their exact meaning never becomes clear until we see or hear them used in a physical or verbal context: "Just look at the wreck that *dog* (mother points at the culprit) has made of my living room!" or "That *dog* Universal Used Cars sold me broke down the second time I drove it," or "Would you like another hot *dog?"*

In reading or writing English, the letters *d-o-g* stand for certain common speech sounds that, put together in this particular order, stand for an object or idea that is in the writer's mind. In Chinese, on the other hand, there is no relation whatsoever between the sound that means *dog* and the pictograph that represents it in writing. As long as an educated Chinese reader or writer is dealing with conventional matters, this absence of a relationship between the spoken and written languages is restricting but not an insuperable obstacle to understanding. When he moves into such fields as nuclear physics or economics, he is seriously handicapped. His language is not capable of the abstractness that modern life demands. Not for nothing have Communist Chinese leaders worked for years to reform their written language.

Your children and you, fortunately, are heirs to an alphabetic system of writing that, though not perfect, certainly is superior to any other system of writing that has yet been devised. A child from Moosehead, Maine, and a child from Window Rock, Arizona, may experience some difficulty at first understanding each other, but unlike comparable Chinese speakers, most of what one says will soon become clear to the other. They will have almost no difficulty at all understanding each other's writing.

PUTTING WORDS IN THEIR PLACES

In neither speech nor writing do words produce meaning simply from being grouped together. The words *that mad shoot, idiots dog you* have little if any recognizable meaning until the words are re-arranged in a pattern that the English-speaking listener or reader expects: "Shoot that mad dog, you idiots!" In our talk, these patterns tend to be simpler and less varied than those we use in writing. Those of us who are native speakers of English may make other kinds of so-called "illiterate" errors (in pronunciation and usage, for ex-ample), but we rarely distort or completely destroy the natural sen-tence patterns of our language, no matter how much or how little education we have had.

In contrast to speaking, writing for most people is not an effortless means of expression, but a laborious one. Writing demands a more precise choice of words. With growing maturity of thought and ac-cumulated experience in writing, our children's sentence patterns in writing tend to be more varied and complex than those they normally speak. However, through grades 4 and 5 at least, writing is done in simple patterns closely resembling those of speech. Punctuation, which we seldom have to consider consciously in speech, must be accurate, as must spelling—which simply does not exist in the spoken language. Consequently, your child finds it much less difficult to express his ideas in speech than in writing. Almost compulsively, he writes: "At the age of ten, my father took the family to see the monkeys in the zoo." In speaking he would, we hope, use the more accurate order: "My father took the whole family to see the monkeys in the zoo when I was ten years old." In conversation, the thought is perfectly clear in either pattern—the grammatical inaccuracy in the first would pass unnoticed by most people. In writing there is no argu-ment as to which would be the preferred form.

Two other characteristics set writing apart from speech and help to explain why most of us often go out of our way to avoid it. First of all, writing is more work in a purely physical sense. Whether one forms words with a pen, pencil, cold chisel, or typewriter, he uses many more muscles than are involved in the act of speaking. If your child is like most children, he may talk all day with no noticeable signs of fatigue. But when he writes, normally little-used muscles of his fingers, arms, shoulders, eyes, and back (not to mention one other set!) are called into action. Unless he is a professional writer-in-training, actual physical fatigue inevitably results. In most of us, physical fatigue interferes with our ability to think clearly and in all but the most strong-willed, it certainly offers a fine excuse for not writing more than is absolutely necessary.

In addition to the physical factor, the care and accuracy demanded of a conscientious writer produces a nervous tension that he would not ordinarily experience as a speaker. The subconscious thought that what he writes may be held against him, in the classroom tomorrow or forevermore, creates a tension that the speaker, whose words dissipate into the surrounding air, usually never feels. This neural fatigue, like the physical, takes its toll of all writers, whether inexperienced adolescents or adult professionals.

People, both the young and the older like us, differ physically and psychologically in their reactions to writing, so that it is not wise to generalize about these factors. Yet neither is it wise for a parent or teacher to overlook these possibilities when a particular child fails to produce the quantity or quality of writing expected. (Malingering, of course, is a different kind of problem, one that belongs more appropriately to the guidance counselor, perhaps, than to the teacher.)

If they thought about it at all, the original inventors of written language probably had in mind no more than a simple and convenient visual substitute for speech. Later men felt a need for a written language in their expanding business, social, and political affairs, but their goal was still not very clearly understood. But in the hands of the storytellers, sages, and poets, the written language has developed into a communication medium that far surpasses its origin, the spoken language. Among the arts it surpasses in influence sound, motion, and representation. Among primitive people, the child knew no more history, science, or poetry than was told him at his hairy parent's knee. His "literature" consisted entirely of stories told him by the "singers" of his tribe or nation. Thanks to the invention of writing, *your* child has at *his* fingertips permanent records of the great (and some not so great) achievements, feelings, and ideas of men for thousands of years.

At this point, a few alarmed parents may suggest that the young, in their insistence on learning via "popular" television, are slipping back into a semiprimitive state. There is no real evidence to support this pessimistic view. In spite of the cheap and often meretricious offerings that spread daily over most of the nation's airwaves, the national level of literacy continues to rise. And the increasing interest of both children and adults in more worthwhile literary works is a matter of record.

Just as the spoken language is effective only when there are alert listeners, so the written language can realize its purpose only when there are competent readers. A writer writes to be read just as a speaker speaks to be heard. "Art for art's sake" is an academic illusion, for however private a writer tries to be, he is always writing for some kind of reader—even if that reader is only himself.

Children, like their elders, write in the hope of being read. They may be passing along information about the world as they see it or they may merely be relieving their inner tensions. In either case, they require an audience. Most of us write *to* or *for* others; few of us often write to or for ourselves alone. This fact neither parent nor teacher should overlook in considering the performance of children in their efforts to master the skill of writing.

WHEN AND HOW
CHILDREN LEARN TO WRITE

3

Much has been written and even more has been said about the way children supposedly learn to write. Actually, a great deal less is known about the process than we like to believe. Most of what we do know that seems important has come not so much from "research" as from the common experience and intuition of tens of thousands of teachers and writers, dating back to Chaucer and before.

Most teachers are agreed, for example, that there is a time that is best for a child to begin receiving formal instruction in written composition, just as there is a time of so-called "reading readiness." This time may be, and generally is, considerably different for each child, though for some it may occur as late as the second or third grade. It is determined partly by the child's ability to retain the visual image of words (vocabulary), his ability to control the physical tools of writing (handwriting), his ability to perceive the world around him and to relate it both to spoken and written language (thought). It is determined by these considerations, plus the inner urge to report what he observes (purpose), and the strength of his desire to imitate the writing that he sees about him (motivation). Thus the child who has been exposed to storytelling and children's books and to parents and friends who write is likely to begin writing at an earlier age and to do so more successfully than a child who has not had these advantages.

Many schools are teaching concomitantly handwriting, writing of sentences, spelling, and reading early in the first grade. In the very beginning, the teacher sets down in manuscript writing what the child dictates. The child copies, then reads what he has written. As he becomes independent in forming manuscript letters and learns the spelling of commonly used words, he writes for himself. Before very long the teacher may lead him into copying notices, notes, and letters, and other communications (including stories and poems) that interest him. The more able students are soon writing independently.

HAVING SOMETHING TO SAY

There is little point, of course, in encouraging a child to begin writing unless he has something to say and the desire to say it in a visual form. So strong is the power of imitation that some children at the age of two or three scribble after the manner of adults they have watched and then "read" what they have intended to say. Many a preschool child asks a parent to print sentences for a letter to Grandmother or Uncle Jim, then copies it in wavering, but legible, fashion. These children are going through an actual writing experience, because they are purposefully conveying a message using conventional symbols. In school, too, we must consider that children are writing whenever they dictate to the teacher what they wish to have written. So writing really begins whenever a child's mind begins to "percolate" and he feels a pressing or even a vague desire to set down his ideas or feelings in the permanent form we call writing.

In the beginning, the child's ideas result largely from direct experience with his environment, though television programs, movies, and juvenile books may make a contribution. The greatest impact results most often from what happens to him and his immediate family, what he and they do; and usually it is about such personal experiences that the beginner at school expresses himself through talking, drawing, and painting, and oftentimes writing. When he writes, he does so because he has thoughts and feelings to express; he has information and opinions he wants to share. His incentive and reward lie in responsive readers (or listeners, if he reads his own product orally) and in the satisfaction of having them understand what he has put on paper and of responding to it.

The child's growing accumulation of experiences and his ability to read more and more on his own produces an increasing store of knowledge about which he may write in the form of personal memoranda, reports, essays, or stories. The need to share his expanding inner world can and should grow ever more urgent; and it is likely to if his teachers, year by year, provide the opportunities for him to write and read his contributions to his classmates, post them on the bulletin board, "publish" them in a school or class anthology, or encourage him to send actual letters through the mail. Also necessary is his teachers' sincere interest in his message, rather than in preoccupation with technical errors.

To be sure, children need to learn the mechanics of writing and should have lessons that teach them how to use their language arts textbook as a reference, which will give them occasional direct instruction on such matters as margins, indentations, capitalization, punctuation, sentence structure, and paragraphing. Such matters are usually learned easily if directly related to the child's own writing, and if the teacher has and takes time to point to the specific spots in his writing where his usage needs improvement.

Perhaps more damage to the child's ultimate desire to express his ideas in writing results from the formal, inflexible demands of an insensitive teacher and of worried adults to write "correctly" and to "make sense" than from any other single cause. Always the teacher must be sensitive to varying degrees of writing aptitude in his pupils, and he must encourage each child to strive for the highest level of achievement possible—numerous, well-organized details and perceptive interpretation on the part of the most apt; much simpler and briefer expression by the slower learner or the disadvantaged. Each child should be helped and encouraged to do as well as he can and should be satisfied by only his best when he submits his finished product.

LISTENING AND READING: SPEAKING AND WRITING

Communication is a two-way street. We get ideas and impressions through the acts of listening and reading; we give out ideas and impressions of our feelings by means of speech and writing. But aside from these two obvious parallels, and the fact that all of these aspects of communication depend almost solely on language, the acts are quite dissimilar in nature.

The child's earliest step in the direction of communication occurs when he listens to, and tries to imitate, the speech sounds around him. But though he may form recognizable words in this experimental stage, he does not really speak "our" language until he has learned also to associate the sound he is making to an understandable object or idea. Children born deaf, of course, learn to use the spoken language only with the greatest difficulty, if at all. Until recently, such unfortunates were mistakenly labeled deaf-mutes and were commonly considered to be mentally defective. Today, thanks to such publicized cases as that of Helen Keller, we know that muteness results in most cases from never *hearing* language, not from mental deficiency. Specialists are inventing and perfecting techniques to teach the deaf, whose only hope used to be to learn to communicate by sign language, an awkward substitute for speaking the language they are condemned never to hear. Only those with unusual drive and intelligence, and with patient families and teachers, were once likely to master the skills of reading and writing. For people with normal hearing, the introduction to language takes place through the act of listening. The subsequent development of their ability to speak, read, and write seems directly related to this initially developed sense.

As the young child grows in his ability to turn his observations and experience first into ideas and then into spoken language, he becomes gradually aware of a relationship between speech and the written (and printed) language. He discovers that certain combinations of marks on paper can represent speech sounds that he recognizes. It is possible, in a limited way, to learn eventually to read visually, without reference to the spoken language, but seemingly the more normal and ultimately more successful method with an alphabetic language such as ours is to begin by relating the spoken to the written symbol. Most schools today combine the visual and the auditory factors in their teaching of reading.

The teaching of writing follows hard on the heels of the teaching of reading, or it may even occur at the same time. For most children, though, skill in the rudiments of reading still precedes their independent attempts at putting their ideas into writing. Just as a child first hears and then copies the sounds of language, so he must see the written forms before he tries to imitate them.

From the time the child has learned to form letters and to order them correctly as words, he is expressing ideas as he labels a picture or copies a sentence he has dictated to the teacher. The following situations and samples from Dyer Street School in Los Angeles will help to make clear how teachers work with children in order to develop the ability to write independently.[1]

A first-grade group learned the physical features of a cow by studying pictures shown by overhead projector. The following description was dictated by members of a group to the teacher, transcribed in manuscript writing, then copied by the more advanced pupils. This was their first experience in writing on lined paper. The less mature children practiced manuscript writing at the board, because they still lacked coordination for writing on lined paper.

> A cow has a muzzle.
> This is her mouth.
> She has no upper teeth.

[1] The samples of children's writing quoted here were contributed by Janice Frost, demonstration and training teacher, formerly at Dyer Street School, Los Angeles Unified School District, Los Angeles, California.

In December the teacher taught her group the proper form for writing a letter. After dictating this letter to the teacher, the children copied it (except that each child changed the first sentence to suit his personal request). The teacher noted in her journal that the group would probably be ready for individual, independent writing of a letter after one more lesson like this first letter-writing experience.

December 10

Dear Santa,
    Please bring me a ball for Christmas. I have been good. We like you very much.

Love,

_____

About a month later, one boy did write his own story. He found most of his words in his word box, a file of the words he had been using in his dictated stories. The occasion was an unusual snowfall low on the mountainside in clear view of the school. This is his story exactly as he wrote it. Notice how little difficulty he had, really, with technicalities.

> We like to play in the snow
> We like to eat snow.
> We have lots and lots of fun.
> It is fun. yum yum
> It is good. yum yum

Some second-grade children wrote independently their individual stories after viewing and discussing a film about a dog and his master. They used their word boxes to help with spelling and were given supplementary help by the teacher. This is a typical story.

> I have a dog at home.
> Her name is Lucky.
> She can run fast.
> I like her.

In another and more advanced second grade, a film about the robin stimulated discussion that resulted in written stories, each one somewhat different from the others. This is one child's story. Note the somewhat uncertain sequence of her ideas, but her excellent sentence sense.

Robin Redbreast

Robbins build nests. They work day and night. They lay little eggs. The eggs hatch into baby Robins. The eggs are blue. The Mother and Father take turns sitting on the nest, and getting food.

The following story written independently by a third-grader shows the advance both in the difficulty of ideas expressed and in the longer and more complicated sentences used.

An Experiment

We had an experiment with a thermometer. Thermometers have red alcohol in them and when you put the thermometer in sunlight or warm water the red alcohol goes up. When you put it in the shade, it goes down.

Though these initial experiences with language appear to follow a fairly fixed order—from listening to speaking to reading and writing —subsequent linguistic development in the normal child consists of almost indistinguishable interweaving of these four basic skills. We absorb new words and sentence patterns from listening and reading; we turn about and use them in speaking and writing as our thoughts require. A logical conclusion from all this seems to be that the better listener and reader a child is, the better speaker and writer he is likely to become. In fact, each of the four language arts reinforces the other three. It seems fairly obvious that a person who exposes himself to a great deal of language in all of its forms is more likely to handle it well than a person who does not.

THE MEDIA OF WRITING

Children today are ordinarily taught manuscript writing before they are taught cursive writing, or handwriting, for sound reasons. The more important, perhaps, is that it is easier for the child to see the relationship between his own manuscript writing and the printed material he is learning to read. If he can also develop a clear, pleasing handwriting later on, so much the better. But in this age of type-writers, printing presses, and other similar machines, his future activity as reader and writer will be mainly concerned with print, not handwriting. Schools are beginning to take note of this fact. For example, in an experiment, begun a few years ago, O. K. Moore of Yale University taught children in a private nursery school from the very beginning to use the typewriter instead of the conventional pencil or pen, reportedly with good results. In some schools, children are being taught to read without formal instruction by means of a computerized typewriter—a machine that speaks to the pupil as well as registers the letters that he presses manually.

Even if experiments such as these prove successful and thus suggest better methods for teaching reading and writing, it will be a good many years before elementary schools in general are equipped with the required machinery, to say nothing of the teachers trained to use it. In the meantime, it is safe to assume that students reaching the upper years of high school will still be expected to turn out respectably handwritten compositions. If, in addition, they have learned to type skillfully, they will have a considerable advantage over their classmates who cannot.

"CREATIVE" WRITING

The term *creative* is not as fashionable today, when applied to writing, as it used to be, particularly at the secondary and college levels. Perhaps because of its excessive use and somewhat fuzzy meaning in the more permissive past, it has come to stand for writing that is too freely self-expressive and undisciplined. The emphasis today, particularly in the colleges, tends toward carefully controlled exposition—writing that explains or analyzes, writing that deals almost exclusively with facts, processes, and ideas.

This emphasis is unfortunate, because the term *creative* should not suggest "lack of self-discipline" but rather the "application of imagination" to whatever problem the writer faces. Creative thinking, in this sense, should be as much a part of the doctoral thesis as of the best-selling novel. The person experienced in writing creatively generally has a clearer sense of structure, of word discrimination, of audience, than the student who has known only formal outlining and the literal cataloging of ideas. Certainly he is a more engaging writer. Few of us will ever become poets, novelists, or playwrights, but we will likely be better writers for having tried.

Most successful elementary school programs afford students continuing experience with imaginative writing. Sometimes the emphasis is districtwide, as in the San Diego City Schools, where an annual volume of children's creative writing is published. (See samples in Chapter 1.) In most schools, it is the result of the efforts of individual teachers to spark creativeness in their pupils. A teacher in Fredonia, New York, for instance, encouraged children to write at home by reading to them stories and verse once submitted by their older brothers and sisters, even their parents. One of her second-graders brought in this bit of verse as his verbal response to seeing a lighthouse turn on its beacons at nightfall.

I saw a lighthouse
  Out all night
Blinking, blinking,
  Blinking out its light.
It looked out
  Over all the sea,
But kept its eye
  On me, on me.[2]

Most secondary schools limit opportunities for imaginative writing to the more gifted, usually as a kind of dessert, often as an elective. This seems a mistake, for the imagination should be stimulated at all levels of ability, even in college. Every child, whatever his ability, should have frequent opportunities to tell stories, to versify, to mate his ideas with the most vividly exact language that he can command. The child thus sensitized to the powers of language cannot help becoming a more effective expositor, provided of course that he has training in the formal aspects of exposition too.

GETTING CHILDREN TO WRITE

Motivation is the art of inducing a person to do willingly that which he otherwise would not likely do of his own accord. It is one of the most essential tools in the teacher's professional kit. The ultimate goal of the teacher, however, is to develop self-motivation in his pupils, for this is the most lasting and desirable kind. Whether child or adult, we are all likely to have our interest stirred by some unusual experience. This happens commonly with professional writers. Robert McCloskey, the popular children's author, reportedly—after watching a policeman halt all traffic to let a mother mallard lead her procession of ducklings across a busy street—wrote *Make Way for Ducklings*. With a child, hearing or reading some verse or a story may trigger similar writing of his own. Teachers report, for instance, that initial experiences in choral speaking often stimulate boys and girls to write creatively on their own. A seventh-grader in Walnut Grove, California, became an almost unquenchable source of verse after her first lessons in choral speaking, even though she had never tried writing poetry before. Almost daily she brought in philosophic, but simple, reflections of her feelings and thoughts, such as this poem, which was one of her first:

---

[2] Commission on the English Curriculum, *Language Arts for Today's Children*. Volume II, NCTE Curriculum Series (New York: Appleton-Century-Crofts, 1954), p. 323. Used by permission of the National Council of Teachers of English.

So very big is the sea,
And I am so very small
That the wonder is that he
Should notice me at all.

Yet when I take my swim
Or play upon the sands,
I shout my joy to him,
And I know he understands.

And when the sky is gray
And the wind is chill,
Something seems to say
He is friendly still.

The sea is so very old
That the earth to him would be,
If all his years were told,
Only a child like me.[3]

The term *motivation,* however, is a blanket term that includes some rather contradictory factors. At one extreme, for instance, the threat of tests, grades, and especially academic failure may be considered powerful motivators of student effort. At another extreme is the lure of sugar coating, the use of irrelevant devices and gimmicks to trick the student into some show of activity. At certain times and with some students, either or both of these approaches may be warranted.

The most effective motivation is that which, using neither threats nor cajolery, awakens in the child (1) an interest in *thinking* about a topic, and (2) an active desire to compose and write down his thoughts. The most successful teacher in this respect actually motivates the whole course of study, rather than a series of individual lessons. By a synthesis of attitudes, personality, knowledge, and teaching methods, he induces frequently in his students the act of purposeful thinking and subsequently the desire to set down their thoughts in writing.

Some of these qualities are born in the teacher, but others are acquirable. Certainly the teacher who is enthusiastic about his material is more likely to elicit interest than is the bored teacher. Similarly, the teacher who is flexible and takes quick advantage of the individual student's current focus of interest is more likely to induce in the child a desire to write well than is the rigid teacher bound to a

[3] Quoted in Mildred Dawson *et al., Guiding Language Learning* (New York: Harcourt, Brace & World, Inc., 1957), p. 472. Used by permission of Harcourt, Brace & World, Inc.

textbook or syllabus. But basic to all else in successful motivation is the teacher's assumption that his students will succeed, not fail, in their efforts at writing. Though a few of the most able students who feel completely secure about their ability may find an acid treatment stimulating, for the majority of students there is no greater stimulus than success—and no greater discourager than failure. With few exceptions, the most effective teachers of writing (or of anything else) are those who build into their students a sense of mounting achievement rather than the frustration of repeated failure.

What is true of the teacher in this respect is true also of the parent. The child at the family dinner table or elsewhere in the home who is included in animated discussion of people, events, and ideas is more likely to write well than the child who experiences only dull silence or, worse, domestic griping and bickering. To a child at the elementary level, the confidence of his parents is especially valuable and generally is well received. Later as the child grows into adolescence, approaching adulthood, his attitude generally makes it increasingly difficult for the parents to avoid nagging and excessive prodding. Yet psychology assures us that at this age too, perhaps more than at any other, it is important for the individual to have the security of a sympathetic audience, the feeling that people are rooting for and not against him.

In passing, we must remark that a positive attitude on the part of either parent or teacher does not imply an entirely uncritical one. Rather, the young person who senses that the critic is with and not against him is much more likely to make good use of the advice and correction offered. The context of the remark, not the remark itself, usually determines the spirit in which the normal young person will receive it.

These observations apply to motivation in general, but there are some suggestions that can be applied to the motivation of writing in particular. The closer a writing assignment lies to the child's personal concerns, usually the more meaningful will be his response to it. Where somewhat general topics are used, preliminary class discussion may help to arouse individual interest that otherwise may be lacking. But whatever method a teacher may employ to spark interest in writing, nothing is more important than the material itself. The writer who is not interested in and concerned with the topic about which he is writing will never produce a good piece of writing. This is true equally of the child or the savant.

WHAT CHILDREN ARE
TAUGHT ABOUT WRITING

4

From the early elementary years through high school into college and beyond, children are presented hopefully with an impressive array of information about writing and composition. Teachers and textbooks talk often and earnestly on subjects as minute as the split infinitive on the one hand and as broad as the great classical principles of rhetoric on the other. And there are almost continuous drill on and consistent attention to such central matters as paragraphing, punctuation, and sentence structure.

The hope is, of course, that enough lore will rub off on your child to make him at least a passable writer by the end of his formal schooling. It is assumed that if he studies enough spelling lists, he will become a better speller. If he is put through enough drill exercises on faulty verb forms or run-on sentences, he will automatically avoid these errors in his own writing. Or if he hears a lecture on coherence in paragraphs, from that time on he will write logically related paragraphs of his own.

Unfortunately, much of this information is presented in lessons that are quite unrelated to the student's own writing. He is asked to study words that he does not himself misspell, or to rewrite faulty sentences that he himself would not have produced in the first place. Or the lesson on paragraph coherence occurs three weeks before he is asked to write a composition long enough to require such coherence.

Even more discouraging, the actual act of writing does not in itself automatically bring about improvement. When a student is asked to write compositions frequently, there is no guarantee that each successive paper will be better than those that preceded it. A recent study of student writing at Dartmouth College showed, in fact, that the writing of seniors contained notably more errors than the writing of sophomores, whose writing in turn contained more errors than that of the freshmen. If this is true of a highly selected and supposedly strongly motivated group of college seniors, what can our expectations be for, say, a group of ninth-graders who have widely varying abilities, interests, and backgrounds?

The problem the teacher of writing faces, at every level, is two-fold: not only must he strike a sensible balance between his presentation of information about composition and the amount of actual student writing that he requires, but he must also make certain that whatever he says "about" composition *has immediate application* to the student's writing. For all kinds of reasons, this is not as simple as it sounds. Perhaps the most complicating fact is that not all students in a class make the same errors or need the same information at any one time. In a given set of compositions, one student may need help with sentence fragments, another with spelling, still another with organization, and so on.

The question of how many student compositions a teacher can or should require will be discussed in Chapter 6. This chapter will indicate and discuss briefly some of the more important aspects of composition that are dealt with in the classroom and textbook in the hope that parents may help a student to absorb them and apply them in his own writing.

"GOOD" WRITING VERSUS "CORRECT" WRITING

A "good" composition is one in which the writer has presented his ideas in logical and effective order, using clear, exact, and vivid language. It may or may not include misspellings, minor grammatical flaws, and questionable usages. Desirably it should not, but if the writer makes his point interestingly and clearly, most readers will consider it "good," regardless.

A "correct" composition, on the other hand, has no misspellings, grammatical flaws, or errors in diction. The writer may or may not present his ideas logically and effectively, in language that is clear, exact, and vivid. If he does not, only a hopeless pedant would set a higher value on a "correct" than on a "good" composition.

Ideally, a composition should present worthwhile content well expressed in mechanically flawless English. But the two factors are not equal. The discerning reader should always give more attention to the content than to the form. We do not turn our backs on the poetry of Chaucer, Shakespeare, the King James translation, simply because they use spellings and grammatical forms that are not considered "correct" today.

Though it seems almost too obvious to mention, it probably should be noted at this point that children at the ninth-grade level should not be held up to standards appropriate to Dartmouth freshmen (or even Dartmouth seniors) either in the content or the mechanics of their writing. Yet ninth-grade teachers—in fact, secondary teachers at every level—are often harsher in their treatment of mechanical flaws than are college teachers.

THE MECHANICS OF WRITTEN ENGLISH

The "correct" writer is the student who has mastered the mechanics of English—spelling, punctuation, grammar, and usage—as set forth in his textbook. His competence in these matters, however, is no guarantee that he can produce a well-organized, meaningful, and interesting composition. For as we have already noted, it is quite possible to say *nothing* beautifully, just as it is possible on occasions to be effective, though illiterate. The sensible person, of course, while giving his chief attention to *what* is said, does not discount the importance of *how* it is said. He devotes a reasonable amount of his time, therefore, to these matters, depending on his particular needs.

Spelling

Realistically considered, English spelling is chiefly a social grace. The language is not noted for its phonetic consistency. Some people are better spellers than others, probably because of superior visual retention. It doesn't seem rational to rank a child spelling prodigy above a nationally important scientist—and we really don't. But for the great bulk of people who fall between these extremes, accurate spelling is important mainly because it is a social expectation.

There is no single avenue to acceptable competence in spelling. It is best taught through a variety of approaches—by study of "demon" lists, by keeping personal lists of troublemakers for systematic review, by developing an interest in words and language in general, wherever they appear.

Least profitable is the study of general word lists, the memorization of affixes, and the too commonly used dictated spelling test. The latter seems especially wasteful because the language is unphonetic in character and because accurate spelling is not an oral problem but is almost entirely a matter of careful proofreading. A child never misspells in speaking; he misspells only in writing. Therefore, instilling in children the dictionary habit is probably the most lastingly helpful single thing a teacher can do.

Punctuation

The use of some marks of punctuation is inescapable. We end a statement with a period, an interrogative sentence with a question mark. The use of other marks is mostly a matter of judgment. When do you use an exclamation mark? When does a comma set off an introductory adverbial modifier? Examine the writing of professionals and you will find the use depends pretty much on the writer's intention.

Punctuation, with few exceptions, is a set of special symbols that we use to show in writing what we would indicate quite naturally in speaking by facial expression, body gesture, or volume and tone of voice. Though a few of the marks are stable (like the commas in addresses and dates), the use of most punctuation is best taught by reference to the spoken language. The punctuation system is not adequate to all of our writing needs, but it is the only system we have to indicate the tone of voice, its intensity, or the pause that separates or emphasizes our ideas in speaking.

Grammar

Nothing is better calculated to stir up a rousing discussion at a PTA meeting than to have a parent ask, "Why aren't our children being taught grammar?" Paradoxically, no topic on the program of a conference of English teachers is more certain to draw a large audience than one dealing in any way with the topic "How to Teach Grammar."

In response to the parent's complaint, it seems safe to assert that most schools today devote a great deal of time to grammar (in some schools, far too much time in the opinion of most authorities), but its presentation is more likely to be keyed to the speaking and writing of a student rather than to be taught formally in the manner that older generations of adults nostalgically recall. Some parents in demanding "more grammar" are using the word in about the same way they do the word *vitamins*. That is, they don't understand actually what either a vitamin or grammar is or how it operates to human advantage. But they do have a vague notion that there is value in it—and therefore, they reason, the more the better! Any parent who doubts this assertion need only examine the school's syllabus or its textbook to be reassured about everybody's concern for grammar.

Yet the truth is that not all is stable in the area commonly referred to as grammar. For the word does not have quite the same meaning today that it had two or more decades ago. That explains, in part at least, why English teachers themselves feel insecure about this particular aspect of their work and seek out any speaker or panel that promises clarification and help.

This book is too short to do more than indicate briefly what has happened to a subject considered so venerable that schools once upon a time were literally known as "grammar schools." At the beginning of the twentieth century, education like all other human concerns became increasingly subject to scientific study and criticism. For half a century, English teachers became increasingly uneasy about the relation of the formal teaching of grammar to the speaking and writing of their students. At the same time, scholars began increasingly to challenge the validity of many of the statements of the traditional grammar books about the English language. Pointing out that English is historically a Germanic, not a Latinate language, they demonstrated conclusively that much of the material traditionally taught is not an accurate description of our language and the way it works. Uncertain what to do, English teachers in the 1920's and 1930's began to abandon the formal teaching of grammar and to substitute so-called *functional grammar.* This meant, in theory, teaching a child the grammatical form he needed at the time he needed to know it. In effect these teachers were teaching usage, not grammar, though this distinction was not clear to them. The result was that the majority of teachers continued to teach, but without strong conviction, the grammar they themselves had been taught. A minority gave up the teaching of grammar altogether, especially following the great influx of disadvantaged students during and following the great Depression of the 1930's.

The turning point was World War II. With its sophisticated communications systems, World War II put an unprecedented emphasis on language skills. Scientific research in language was stimulated, and out of the war came not only scholars but mathematicians and computer technicians as well who were interested in discovering what the English language really is and how it really operates. Shortly after the war, new and seemingly radically different descriptions of English grammar were advanced. Today, as a result, the teacher of English is offered not one, but several grammars of English from which to choose. If he dares or is uninformed, he may continue to offer his students the traditional grammar of English. If he dares and is sufficiently informed, he may offer either *structural, transformational, generative,* or *tagmemic grammar.*[1] And the end of theorizing and research is not yet in sight!

Whatever he chooses to do in the next few years, the English teacher is bound to find himself caught in the middle of a great debate. Added to this confusion are the studies that preponderantly claim to

[1] For a detailed description of the several grammars of English, see Miriam Goldstein, *The Teaching of Language in Our Schools* (New York: The Macmillan Company, 1966), a companion volume in this series.

show that there is little or no relationship between a knowledge of formal grammar (of whatever variety) and a child's ability to speak and write English with facility. Is it any wonder that the teacher is confused? And if the teacher is confused, what of the parent or layman who, in general, is almost entirely ignorant of these advances in our knowledge of our native language! It might be noted, incidentally, that college teachers of English are not notably less confused than teachers of English at the elementary and secondary levels.

By way of reassurance, however, several observations may be offered on the subject of grammar:

1. For children who have some ability to think abstractly, an understanding of the structure and forms of the English language is important, however they are presented. Some schools, in fact, offer grammar not as a tool for reading and writing, but primarily as a part of liberal education.

2. If we accept the validity of the many studies, both American and British, that question the effect of formal grammatical knowledge upon a person's ability to speak and write well, then we should be thankful for teachers independent enough to devote more time to instruction in speaking, writing, and the study of good literature than to endless grammatical drills. Interestingly, in this connection, with the possible exception of oral spelling drills, no aspect of the study of English requires less effort of the teacher than the formal teaching of "traditional" English grammar.

3. Psychology assures us that children at an early age know, for all practical purposes, all of the elements of grammar needed to express themselves effectively in adult life. This, however, does not take into consideration their knowledge of acceptable English usage, which is discussed next.

Usage

Many people who speak of grammar are in reality talking about *usage*. Grammar deals with the predictable structures and word forms that characterize our language, spoken or written. Usage deals mainly with the exceptions to these matters, but it also deals with the changing status of particular words in differing times, places, and situations. As we have already noted, a child entering school has learned by imitation most of the essential grammar of the language. What he has not yet learned is to distinguish among the different kinds of English and to use the kind that is clearest and most appropriate to his purpose.

There are three major kinds of English in more or less common use: informal English, formal English, and nonstandard English. The first two, informal and formal, together form the *standard* level of English, the level used by educated people. The *nonstandard* level is used by people who have not had much education or whose education has failed to influence their speech and writing.

In the three kinds of English, most of the words and grammatical forms are the same. The differences exist in the uses of certain words and constructions, and in the formality of tone. For example, in substandard English, which is almost solely a spoken English, one hears expressions like *ain't, busted* (for *broken*). At the other end of the scale, formal English, which is ordinarily found only in writing intended for very special and important occasions, uses big and unusual words, sentences that are carefully structured and often complex, and language that has an unmistakably bookish tone.

For educated speakers and writers, the most generally useful of the three kinds is informal English, which avoids the objectionable characteristics of the substandard, but is less exacting than the formal. It is the English that educated people ordinarily use in their personal and public affairs, though it too varies in formality from the easy, intimate conversations of the family circle to the writing found in business letters and much literature.

When children understand that there is not one, but several kinds of English, each suitable for its purpose, and that the choice of which to use is entirely up to them, they respond much more readily to the teacher's recommendations. For, looking about them, they cannot fail to observe that the traditional notion of "one correct English" simply does not describe the way even educated people use the language.

The problem of teaching usage places the teacher in somewhat of a dilemma. Clearly he is interested in encouraging all of his students to choose standard over nonstandard usages in their speech and writing. In doing so, he is often battling family, neighborhood, and community standards. If teachers attack and counter the problem on subjective, emotional grounds—"Nice people don't say 'He don't'" versus "But my father says it, and what's wrong with my father?"— they will not make much progress in raising the student's language sights. But if teachers remain calmly objective and present the facts about the various levels of usage, leaving the decision up to the individual (where indeed it belongs), most students are sensible enough to make, or to want to make, the desired choices.

Because encouraging students to change from nonstandard to standard usages is largely a matter of breaking and reforming habits, habits of long standing, drills on specific items may sometimes, but not necessarily, be useful in addition to the student's strong personal desire to change. Drills that are unrelated to the student's purpose, however, are not likely to have much effect upon his habits of speech and writing.

Informal English is the most generally useful of the three kinds of English, and the teacher's main goal should be to help his students learn to use it with comfort and accuracy. Whether in conversation with family and friends or in writing business letters, school assignments, or papers for more general audiences, the student needs to be familiar with and to use good informal English. If his goal, however, is college and eventually a responsible business, political, or professional career, he will need also to be acquainted with the more precise uses of formal English. Because formal English is mainly written English and has a more exacting vocabulary and more complex sentence structures, it is the most difficult level for most students to master. On the other hand, formal English is a level that many students may never have occasion to use, especially if they are not college-bound.

It is probably important to note at this point that, in spite of what many people believe, standards in language are not established by an elect group of experts, either scholars or dictionary editors. Standard English is the language of educated people, whether they are lawyers, clergymen, teachers, or diplomats. It is the language that educated people expect to find spoken or written in both their everyday and special affairs. It is the language that is clear, appropriate to the occasion. And when it is also lively, so much the better.

WRITING THE "GOOD" ENGLISH SENTENCE

There has never been much agreement among scholars about the exact definition of the sentence, though on one point they are fairly unanimous—the sentence is the basic structure of thought. When a child puts two or more words together in a pattern that sounds familiar and that makes sense to those around him, he has begun to use sentences, even if it is something as simple as "Me want" or "Bad doggie." By the same token, when he combines words this simply or in more complex structures, we consider that he has really begun to think.

To many people (and unfortunately this includes many inadequately trained English teachers), a good sentence is merely one that contains no mechanical errors. They apparently assume that if the form of a sentence is flawless, the thought will automatically take care of itself. Thus a child who writes nonsense with grammatical "correctness" not infrequently gets a higher grade than the child who is bubbling with important ideas but has trouble with commas, spelling, or sentence fragments. Some children, indeed, come out of their English classes with no understanding at all that the best sentences grow out of the clearest, most imaginative thinking, that even the best sentences can be improved, and, finally, that matters of structure, proper subordination and emphasis, and coherence are far more important than mechanical errors—unwanted as these are.

The preceding assertion is not intended to encourage faulty writing. It does attempt to suggest that in judging student writing, the quality of the ideas expressed should be the primary concern and should account for the bulk of the credit. Students seriously interested in self-improvement tend, as they progress in school, either to outgrow most of their language faults or to become self-corrective—with the exception of those who possess a natural streak of "carelessness" or who simply do not have what it takes. Carelessness has to be dealt with by the child's parents as well as by his teachers; it is only incidentally the concern of his English teacher. Carelessness, after all, is not English. Sheer lack of ability is not a subject that we need to discuss here, except to note that unfortunately it does exist.

The most important aspect of English grammar is that which deals with the structure of the sentence, technically called *syntax*. English is essentially a syntactical language. It expresses meaning mainly through its sentence patterns, and only to a limited extent through inflected word forms. That is why the study of Latin is not the royal road to competence in English that some people like to assume.

Roughly 90 per cent of English sentences follow the basic subject-verb or subject-verb-object pattern. But the other 10 per cent are important because they contribute variety and emphasis to our writing. Learning to recognize and use these patterns effectively should be one of the student writer's chief concerns. But again it must be pointed out that the pattern of a sentence grows out of the thought it expresses and from its relation to the other sentences around it. Good sentences result from sound thinking.

Most of us were brought up on the definition "A sentence is a group of words with a subject and predicate that expresses a complete thought." There are weaknesses in this traditional definition, easily demonstrated by two easily checked observations: (1) The best writers often write sentences that lack subject, verb, or both, and educated speakers think nothing of using such sentences: "Stop!" or "Quiet!" as in commands, or more frequently in answering questions, "What do you want for lunch?" "Tomato and lettuce sandwiches." "With mayonnaise?" "Yes." (2) On the other hand, a great many sentences do *not* express complete thoughts within themselves, even though they contain subject and verb. "They reported what happened." This is grammatically a complete sentence, but it does not tell us who *they* are, *what* happened, or *when* it happened. That is, this single sentence does not tell us these essential matters, though it is likely the sentences before and after it make everything quite clear.

It is in the matter of sentence study that the new scientific grammars differ most conspicuously from traditional grammar. In the formal study of traditional grammar, the chief emphasis was placed on *analysis,* on *breaking* a sentence down and classifying its parts (and often on model sentences in what many times turned out to be Rube Goldberg-like concoctions!). By contrast, the newer grammars are concerned with synthesis. In generative grammar, for instance, the child is acquainted with the basic pattern of English sentences and then encouraged to produce (that is, "generate") good sentences of his own.

The newer grammars are neither simpler nor easier to learn than the traditional grammar that was set down by eighteenth-century scholars and that has been our sole approach to the study of English in the two centuries since. The new grammars, however, do have the virtue of honesty—they are the product of scholars who have looked at English with scientific detachment and have set out to describe how the language, as they see it, works. Unlike the eighteenth-century grammarians, modern scholars are not handicapped by sentimental attachment to the ancient and moribund languages of Latin and Greek. Instead they are looking at the living English that we speak and write today. Though English depends less upon grammar than any other of the world's major languages, except Chinese, it is still a highly complex language. Any description of its grammar is bound to be complex.

Whatever the approach, the main focus of any grammar is the sentence, however it is defined. People begin early and continue to use sentences all of their lives. In their everyday affairs, they accomplish this quite independently of the "study" of grammar. But for cultural, if not for practical reasons, any person who aims at a "higher" education has no rational excuse for not exploring thoroughly the structure and operation of his native language according to some orderly system. If he requires a practical reason, the demand for precision in scholarly, professional, and important business writing often calls for ability to recognize and rearrange the structure of all parts of a sentence.

We remind you at this point of the PTA member who asks, "Why doesn't the school teach more grammar?" And we call attention to his generalization. There are some children who simply do not have the mental equipment to make sense of even the simplest of the abstractions of grammar, though for their purposes they may speak English well enough. There is a larger group for whom high school is the terminus of their education. They are students who for vocational reasons are very much interested in learning standard informal usage but are not much concerned, if at all, with theoretical matters. They are capable intellectually of grasping the simpler principles of grammar, but intensive exposure is more likely to result in antagonistic attitudes toward the language than to produce notable improvement in its use. There is no evidence to show that detailed study of grammar helps these children. A smaller group at the top, however, find the study of grammatical theory not only interesting, but to an unknown extent they probably apply it to their own writing. Whatever their assessed or real ability level, however, most children need habits of good usage more than they need knowledge of grammar.

In other words, there is no easy answer to the often voiced plea for the teaching of *more* grammar. For improved writing, most young people probably need and will profit more from the better teaching of good speech, composition, and literature than from an intensive study of grammar. In this respect, teachers today are faced too often with an unsolvable dilemma when they set up their courses of study in English. What it boils down to is—"to study grammar, or not to study grammar"—and if we do, how much, and *which?*

THE ROLE OF THE PARAGRAPH

Important as paragraphing is and much as is said about it in the textbooks, most young writers have considerable trouble learning to write good paragraphs, and not without reason!

For one thing, when books and teachers talk about paragraphs they usually have in mind only one kind—the logically developed expository paragraph. This type of paragraph occurs mainly in rather formal material that few children, and not a great many adults, find very often in their general reading. In fiction, advertising, and newspapers, which are for most people the main sources of reading materials, the paragraph indentation serves an entirely different purpose from that in expository writing. It is not really surprising, therefore, or rare, to find students whose idea of paragraphing is to indent every third or fourth sentence, "because it looks better that way." What this means, of course, is that it looks more familiar to them; it is the only kind of paragraphing they have been exposed to in most of their reading.

More misleading, perhaps, is the way in which many English teachers approach the writing process. Instead of stressing the "wholeness" of a composition, their entire emphasis is on the "parts." They see writing as a simple process of choosing words, putting words into sentences, grouping sentences into paragraphs, and of stringing enough paragraphs together, and at the end of the process, presto, a composition! This sequence seems logical enough, but an experienced writer who has carefully examined his *modus operandi* can testify that this is not the way writing takes place.

The good writer does not start with individual words that he puts together like building blocks. He starts with a subject, an idea of some complexity and (to him, at least) of importance. His first step is to break this large subject down into its main parts, which will help him to determine many of his paragraph divisions. Not until he has organized his thinking in this way (in more important compositions even to the extent of writing down a formal outline) is he ready to deal with sentences and words. Good expository paragraphing is, then, largely a matter of organizing and structuring one's major ideas on a given subject.

The ability to plan and write good expository paragraphs is especially important to the child who is headed for college, because he will be asked to write a great many formal expository papers, not just in English, but in all of his college courses. The upper elementary years are not too early for such children to begin developing their recognition of topical sentences and especially of the importance of supporting details. Conversely, an understanding of the structure of a formal paragraph is as important to a reader as it is to a writer.

This chapter has presented, much too briefly, some of the major matters that your child will be concerned with in learning to write his native language. It has tried to place some of these items, grammar and good sentences, for instance, in perspective. How much you can help your child with these rather technical aspects of writing depends, of course, upon your own skill and experience as a writer. If your knowledge is limited to what you yourself learned from textbooks a generation or more ago, you will be wise to let the teacher do the teaching of these important matters. You can perhaps be most helpful by making sure that your child is provided with well-written books and magazines and by encouraging him to read them. If by chance he permits you to read what he writes, your role should be that of the interested and sympathetically critical reader. But remember that children are normally and notoriously allergic to parental criticism— so find less to criticize than to praise in your child's writing!

5

If having something to say is the starting point of good writing, then certainly the English teacher must give considerable time and attention to helping his students discover the ideas and impressions that lie untapped in even the least talented minds. Not only must he become fully aware of what they *want* to talk and write about, but he must go a giant step further and infer what they *can* think and write about. This is an important distinction, because left to their own devices, children quite naturally choose to write on the least resistant topics. Guided toward more challenging subjects, as likely as not they discover new interests that can open all kinds of doors.

It is no more possible to generalize about the interests of children than it is of adults. Like the rest of us, children too are individuals. A teacher—on the basis of past experience—might state confidently, for instance, that the care and breeding of pets is a unique interest of ninth-grade students, then find in the next moment a *third-grade* hamster-raising specialist or a *twelfth-grade* homing pigeon fancier to confound his generalization. Yet in spite of the inevitable exceptions, there is a recognizable pattern in children's interests, as veteran teachers and parents can attest.

As a beginning writer, the child is likely to be a realist, reflecting his microcosmic world with sometimes painful clarity, examining it with simple logic. He likes to talk about his adventures—the Thanksgiving trip to Grandmother's, holding the new baby, the skinned knee. He talks about family secrets in a candid way that would cause his parents extreme anguish if they knew. (Teachers, though they take no "Hippocratic" oath, fortunately have a well-developed sense of decency about this sort of thing!) He reports on his playmates, his home, his neighborhood. And, of course, there are always the pets. He writes lucidly and directly about these things, presenting his world as he sees it, with little or no attempt to ornament or change it. All this is true of "typical" beginning writers; but there are those whose parents have steeped them in imaginative folk tales and stories of fantasy—classic and modern; and many of these children write of make-believe situations and characters and concoct intriguing though simple plots.

A child in the elementary school gains ever-widening horizons as he learns of the far away and the long ago, reads books of fiction and fact, and learns to use reference books in his pursuit of knowledge. Alert teachers contrive to take advantage of situations that give reason for him to write reports, explanations, and stories featuring the knowledge that he as an individual has sought and acquired. Thus many a child goes into the junior high school with attitudes and abilities favorable to continued purposeful writing.

However, when the child enters the junior high school years (normally at age twelve) and his sophistication begins to develop, evidences of shrewdness, caution, and affectation are likely to show in his writing. Social pressures from without and the inner personal worries that mark the onset of adolescence begin to affect him. Though some children continue to report their world with innocence, others—and especially boys—begin to hide themselves in sketchy, generalized compositions that reveal little or nothing about their thoughts.

Still others, at this stage, show a strong tendency to return to fantasy, but not to the innocent imaginings of early childhood. The child who only a few years before unself-consciously reported the latest bitter family quarrel as if it were a normal part of life, now is likely to try to remake the world by writing about a happy family situation that he wishes were true. Or the child from an economically poor home writes nonchalantly about cars, clothes, and other advantages that he yearns for but is ashamed to admit are not his (though girls, perhaps, are more likely than boys to engage in this kind of verbal daydreaming). In many boys, imagination is stirred by a dream world of monsters and supermen.

The interests of high school writers are more difficult to generalize. Many children by this time have begun to develop hobbies of various kinds: sports, cooking, cars—and with the girls, of course, boys and dating. (Though sex has certainly been a topic of private discussion beginning in the junior high school years, it seldom rears its head, ugly or otherwise, in the public writing of adolescents, except very indirectly in the romanticizing of some precocious girls.) At this stage, manifestations of the growing sense of independence, "gripes," are likely to appear often in their writing; the ego is probably stronger and blinder than at any other age. The child resents classmates, parents, teachers, school, community—anything and everything that tends to restrict him or to challenge his emerging, but still insecure, sense of self. The class composition, the editorial column, or letters to the editor section of the school newspaper may serve as an outlet for these resentments. Experienced teachers understand and make allowances. Unfortunately, many parents and laymen become unduly excited, especially when some more aggressive (and often more competent) students carry their complaints to the local press.

In the later years of high school, as students sense the end of their childhood and begin to think about jobs, marriage, technical training, or college, their individual concerns and ambitions become increasingly apparent in the composition topics about which they choose to write. A substantial number of students at this age, overwhelmed by pressures in their personal lives, find in writing for the teacher, if not an ideal, at least a somewhat comforting safety valve. Not uncommonly he is the only confidant some students have. The wise teacher watches for these "distress signals" and does not reject them. In a sense, he recognizes them as a compliment, for they are testimony to the child's confidence in him. Here again the wisdom and expertness of the teacher are crucial: Shall the child be failed for working out his tensions rather than standing up precisely to the demands of the assignment? This is a decision that every teacher faces, and not infrequently.

Fortunately many teachers of English have some exposure to psychology and guidance in either their preservice or inservice training; consequently they realize that it is important for children to have safety valves, such as writing "shockers" or "articles of protest." Such teachers learn to read between the lines and gain an understanding of the turmoil that such papers reflect; they believe that the message is often far more significant than the writer's inaccuracy in using the technicalities of English. Those English teachers who have not had courses in guidance are almost sure to number among their colleagues one or more guidance teachers, who can help them understand the needs and the problems that students' papers often reveal.

All that has been said so far applies mainly to the average, normal, numerically most common youngster. But there are others to be considered. There are, naturally, children of less than normal intelligence and ability, weak both in ideas and imagination, for whom writing is an agonizing and unsettling experience. These children, for the most part (though who can predict surely in what number and to what degree?), will spend their lives communicating almost entirely in speech, not writing. How much writing and of what kind should the teacher demand of them? Should they be held strictly to a single, absolute standard? These are questions that old hands at teaching often find more difficult to resolve than do the less experienced.

And what about that other special group, the so-called "gifted" children? While their practical-minded fifth-grade classmates are dealing with everyday situations and ordinary facts, these children have already begun to discern and to explore in their writing the meanings of human relationships and of complex ideas like the conservation of natural resources. Or, in twelfth grade, while less gifted classmates are considering job possibilities or marks high enough to permit college entrance, these precocious young people are pursuing the language of higher mathematics or examining the writings of a Hopkins, an Eliot, or a Brecht. Are their composition needs identical with those of their less gifted classmates? Or is the difference merely in degree and not in kind?

If a school uses a "track system," with specially designed programs for the slow, the average, and gifted groups, some of the problems arising from such human differences may be partly solved. But only some and only partly! Besides, new problems of human relationship and personal development are created. Statistics are not available as to the number of schools in the country using ability grouping on a large scale. It seems fair to estimate that half or more of the schools still operate, for all practical purposes, as single-track schools. This is particularly true of elementary and junior high schools, though many now are adding special services (remedial reading specialists, guidance personnel, coordinators, and other consultants) to help care for the needs of typical students, whether average, retarded, or gifted. We should say, perhaps, that the ability grouping that characterizes a multiple-track system has not been found to be an unqualified success. It has been shown that children of superior ability gain human understanding and ability to appreciate the contributions of less able children who have integrity, willingness to work, reliability, and who may be particularly apt in music, art, dramatics, or sports. Separated into special groups, they miss this important human experience.

But "special services" do not change the basic teaching problem in classes whose pupils may range from the retarded to the genius. The teacher of writing faces, in these classes, a particularly complex task in setting up meaningful and exciting composition assignments that will encourage each child to perform to the best of his ability. Happily, the more expert teachers of English do just that!

WRITING ON ASSIGNED TOPICS

Thus far we have been talking about the natural interests of children—the kinds of topics they turn to if left to their own devices. But most compositions are written, it seems safe to assume, on topics if not assigned, at least initiated, by the teacher. Most students actually prefer to have the topic furnished them. A completely free assignment like "Write a composition for tomorrow on *any* topic you choose" paralyzes the majority of young writers.

It is not that any one of these students lacks interesting and worthwhile material to write about; it is simply that the directions are so formless that in their inexperience young writers have trouble focusing on a workable topic. The purpose of the writing is not stated, so that for most of the students, "purpose" becomes little more than fulfilling an obligation and escaping a zero in the teacher's record book. Such a purpose is not likely to produce good writing, and seldom does.

Unhappily, too many composition assignments of this general type are handed out by inadequately trained and unimaginative teachers.

At the other extreme from the teacher who gives his pupils little or no direction in choosing topics is the one who assigns narrowly restricted topics without reference to students' interests or abilities or backgrounds. "For tomorrow write a 500-word composition on Hamlet's father's ghost." Any normally intelligent high school student might well ask why he should have to write such a paper. A few of the more gifted may turn out charming or even perceptive compositions on the topic, but the bulk of the class will write incomprehensible gibberish. To encourage the writing of gibberish is to teach bad writing that someday must be unlearned.

The effective teacher gives composition assignments that take into account both the children's interest *and* their abilities. He prepares for the assignment with discussion of the general subject from which the topic is to be drawn. In this discussion the purpose of the composition should become clear. He will make the actual assignment definite, yet flexible enough to allow for varying individual viewpoints. He will allow pupils to ask as many questions as necessary to clarify in their minds the purpose and limits of the assignment. He will do all that he can to make the assignment meaningful to each member of the class.

Such an assignment challenges a child to think for himself, yet bolsters his confidence by pointing out some directions in which he can go. Out of a ninth-grade class discussion of family relationships, based on the reading of *The Yearling* or *Tom Sawyer,* should come twenty-five compositions on twenty-five different aspects of the problem, each reflecting the personal experience and honest opinions of the writer. But if the preliminary discussion is too formalized, if the assignment is too narrowly restricted, if the teacher is unsympathetic to interrogation, then the result may easily be twenty-five carbons of a stereotyped viewpoint that would have been better left unexpressed.

Whether one views classroom composition writing merely as practice for adult writing situations or as an immediate means of developing the child's powers of perception and thought, it has no value unless it is meaningful and its purpose clear to the writer. Either it must be based on the child's established interest or it must generate a new interest, in the same manner as learning to dive less flatly or to play the piano with a lighter touch. The clever teacher (and parent, too, when the opportunity offers) is the one who understands fully the power of motivation and searches for ways of creating interest in writing that normally a child will not find for himself. In this regard, John Dewey once noted, "Having to say something is a different matter from having something to say."

ALL-SCHOOL WRITING

Most parents—and many teachers, too, regrettably—have come to regard the teaching of writing as the sole responsibility of the teacher of English. No professionally minded English teacher will argue the fact that the bulk of formal instruction and practice does lie within his province—and he wants it that way. But if other subject matter teachers and parents do not accept a reasonable share of the responsibility for the child's applying what he has learned at all times, the English teachers' efforts are largely wasted.

Actually, most children are asked to do, quantitatively, in their history, science, and other courses more writing than they are in the English class. Too often the subject matter teacher issues "blanket" assignments with no thought that he is literally inviting bad writing. The social studies teacher demands long outlines of material read, and excessively long and dull reports of generalized historical events. The science teacher asks for paraphrases (erroneously called "reports") of material only partly read and learned, instead of encouraging original reports of creative thinking. Because "facts" are the main concern of such teachers, they are likely to accept all kinds of slovenly writing. And they evaluate learning of facts by giving objective examinations, because their concern, understandably, is for the subject matter and not for flagrant signs of inept writing.

What is even more deplorable, in schools that employ inadequately trained personnel, the teachers are often no better writers than the students themselves. Thus they are in no position to comment helpfully or to grade fairly the writing they assign. If the blame for this sorry condition could be pinpointed—and it probably cannot be— the colleges who graduated these teachers, the state agencies who licensed them, and the local authorities who hired them must share it in common.

Here and there, a college (and even, in a few instances, a high school) has recognized this problem and has made a valiant effort to enlist the cooperation of *all* of its faculty in the endless effort to improve the quality of undergraduate writing. The initial burst of enthusiasm has, sometimes, reportedly produced favorable results. But as time wears on and the effort and time needed to coordinate and maintain the interest of geology, economics, and psychology professors become greater, the English department becomes disillusioned and gives up the battle. The fact that even some members of college English departments refuse to accept responsibility for the writing of their students is, of course, no incentive for their colleagues in other departments to do so.

What is true of college English departments in this respect is also true, though to a lesser extent, in many high schools. Here and there a high school makes a short-lived effort to maintain an "all-school" approach to the improvement of student writing. Only at the elementary level, where a single teacher is responsible for all subject matter as well as for the teaching of writing, are we likely to find this kind of approach followed consistently. Yet even at this level, with its built-in, natural advantages, the effectiveness of the effort is open to some question, because most elementary teachers have had a minimal training in composition in their own college work.

This lack of integration of subject matter and writing training is most unfortunate, particularly at the higher levels of high school and in college. Many students find in their subject matter fields the ideas and experiences that are most likely to elicit good writing. This is especially true of the social sciences, where outlining and paraphrasing so often serve as the mere handmaidens of reading. No simple solution to this whole problem seems possible. However, in the English class, some practicable steps toward solution might frequently be (1) to encourage each student to select composition topics in the subject matter areas of greatest interest to him, (2) to have him write as if he had been a participant or observer of any events or discoveries he reports (thus he would tend to paraphrase little if at all), or (3) to ask him to compare conditions at the time and place of major concern with those prevalent at earlier or later dates, in other locales, or under similar conditions. That is, students should be encouraged to make personal evaluations of and to react to the data they collect for their writing.

One way of getting students to think through the subject matter for their themes is to set up small committees to deal with each of several topics such as the effects of the Crusades on West European culture, dangers in using antibiotics without a prescription, practical values of landing on the moon, or actual social conditions in England at the time *Oliver Twist* was written. Time is set aside for small-group discussion (each committee forming a group) to explore points of view, possible sources of information, and likely subtopics to serve as foci for individual papers. The discussion tends to personalize the topic for each student so that he is encouraged to seek data to support and clarify the points he wishes to present. His fellow committee members become prospective judges who evaluate the authenticity and logic of his presentation. (His English teacher might be relatively uninformed on such specialized subjects but could objectively decide whether the paper reflected thorough preparation, substantiating facts gained from reliable sources, logical development, appropriate vocabulary used to make meanings clear, and other characteristics of writing that convey ideas effectively to the reader.)

THE SCIENCE "BOOM" AND WRITING

The burgeoning emphasis upon science has had its effect upon the teaching of English, as it has upon all other school offerings. In a culture that is saturated with respect for and faith in the "scientific process," this is hardly to be wondered at. Whereas only a few decades ago humanistic scholars looked "down their noses" at their colleagues in the science departments, "research" is a common term today among students of literature—and the capitulation has gone so far that even poetry is being offered in machine-like programed "sets."

The influence of this current commitment to science is felt in the composition program in a variety of ways—in the attempt to make new concepts of grammar functional in the writing process, in the concern with the semantic properties of words, and even to a marked degree in the choice of topics for writing.

Forty years ago, it was still fairly common for graduating seniors to be required to write a formal "literary" paper or to deliver an equally formal oration upon some topic from the humanities. The oration has fallen by the wayside. Today it is more common for schools to require a "research paper" (or a "resource theme") from at least its college-bound students. A large portion of these papers deal with topics from the sciences. In all of them, the main emphasis is no longer on rhetoric; it is on the careful selection, organization, and reporting of facts. For better or worse, ringing rhetoric on "The Glory of Mankind—His Conscience" has given way to the precise, orderly report on "The Mating Habits of the Auk"—with only slight exaggeration.

Concern about the quality (or as charged, the lack of it) in much student writing has resulted in a lively side debate about the merits of the "research theme." Many college teachers have condemned this particular kind of writing, urging the high school teachers to concentrate upon "the fundamentals of writing" and to leave the specialized forms to them. On the other hand, many college students who did not receive this special training in high school report that though almost every department in the college requires such papers, at no point are they taught specifically how to prepare them.

Both sides have their points. The critics are certainly right when they point to high school "research themes" that are mere rehashes of encyclopedia articles, dashed off at the eleventh hour—and often graded "excellent" by teachers so overburdened that they cannot look beyond the bulk of the writing, the neat typing, the impressive bibliography. In one reported instance, an *eighth-grader* who handed in an 80-page typed social studies report, copied almost verbatim from her sources, received an *A*. Her classmates who had put at least *some* thoughtful effort into their much briefer and for the most part handwritten, more difficult to read papers received substantially lower grades.

Yet to condemn teaching the process of collecting, organizing, and reporting materials in clear English, even at the elementary level in an age that places such a high value on science, just doesn't make sense. Though he does so obviously at a much less sophisticated level, the fifth-grader is as capable as the professionally trained entomologist of observing the antics of the ant—and of reporting what he sees. The fault does not lie with the assignment or with the student, but with the teacher who fails, first, to show the student exactly how to do the job, and second, to make clear the difference between plagiarism and honest reporting.

Properly taught, the research theme offers a ready-made context within which students can be taught such necessary skills as reading for information, notetaking, library research, organization of ideas, and more. No one expects a high school student, however talented, to produce a doctoral thesis. There is no reason, though, why he should not learn in simple form the research process that he will be expected to use in many areas of his future endeavor. To urge postponing until college the introduction of the student to the research process is about as sensible as barring a child from talking until he is six years old on the premise that he is then better able to learn to talk.

When a child is assigned a research theme to write, the important responsibility of the parent is to keep him "honest" and to keep him working under his own steam. Where possible, the parent should guide the child to the facts but not supply them; discuss possible sources of information—the encyclopedia or *World Almanac,* the reference librarian at the public library, the knowledgeable neighbor to be interviewed, the downtown Bureau to be queried, the files of old newspapers in the "library" at the *Evening Star.* Above all, the parent should impress upon him the importance of initiative, of persistence, of thoughtful conclusions—let the grades fall where they may! A parent who is so ambitious for his child that he tries to do the work for him is merely preparing his child for a bad shock later on in business or in college.

One absolute essential for out-of-school work on compositions is that the parent help his child to find a place and a time for study that is free of interruption and disturbance. If home is necessarily a crowded, noisy place, then the child should be helped to find a quiet spot where he can work well—at Grandmother's, at a classmate's home, at a study center set up at the YMCA or other public place. The requirements of writing cannot compete with the excitement of television or the normal jostle of the family living room.

LITERATURE AS A SOURCE OF IDEAS FOR WRITING

No hard and fast statement can be given about the use of literature as a source for topics in composition. Certainly the college-bound student should be able to take a literary work and discuss its ideas in terms of the writer's purpose as well as of his own experience. To expect a student who can barely read even the simplest materials to assume the role of "literary critic" seems rather ridiculous. Yet there is no reason why even this student cannot react intelligently in writing to literary works that are appropriate to his understanding level and his interests.

Next to personal experience, reading is our richest source of ideas. From it we obtain practically the only information that is available about the generations of people who preceded us on this planet. From it, too, we get much of our understanding of ourselves as human beings. Some teachers, unfortunately, regard each book or other literary work as a kind of museum specimen, and the reaction they demand of the child is the cut-and-dried ritual of the formal "book report."

In some ways children are like Pavlov's dogs. After they burn their hands enough times on a hot stove, they learn to avoid the stove. After they have been penalized enough times by having formal reports assigned for each book they read, many children (then, and later as adults) learn to avoid books—even when no teacher is around to require a report! We do not, as adults, read books in order to write formal reports on them. We do like to discuss the books we read, however; and if we really like them, we may even talk and write to our friends about them.

If the literature read in school makes any kind of impression upon young people (and we know that upon most of them it does), then it cannot fail to be a source of many of their ideas. A good deal of their writing, therefore, should center upon the people, the events, the problems about which they read *as well as* those they meet face to face in the world of actual experience. The best writing occurs when the reading and the living experience are congruent.

PLAGIARISM AND THE STUDENT WRITER

What a comfort it would be not to feel required to touch formally upon the subject of plagiarism in student writing! But unhappily there are students who, with premeditation or by accident, do plagiarize. Worse, there are parents who encourage them to do so, directly by example—or unintentionally by subjecting them to unbearable pressures: to make the "right" college, to bring home a "good" report card, or most commonly, perhaps, to escape a "failing" grade.

Some of this plagiarism is innocent and perhaps unavoidable where students substitute subconsciously remembered words and ideas for original thought and expression. Less easily rationalized is the plagiarism of the child who, because of poor planning or because of unreasonable assignments, pursues the easy course—handing in work copied from that of classmates or even from published sources. This is not the place to discuss the implications of the apparent fact that this kind of dishonesty is more prevalent among college-age students than among those in the lower schools. But it is a matter that every responsible parent—and college teacher—should ponder long and deeply.

Not to be pardoned at all, of course, is the student who sets out deliberately to plagiarize either for "kicks" or for personal advancement. Such students (and parents who abet them) are not at all interested in the honor that such grades can produce. This kind of dishonesty is on a par with robbing a cash register or committing a fraud. It is, in fact, a crime punishable by law, though at the school level it seldom if ever finds its way to the courts. One can hardly discount the analogy, however, that the tree grows in the same direction as the twig is bent.

At times, to be sure, the problem rests as much with pedagogy as with morality. In any subject field a teacher with poor preparation or an impossible student load may even encourage the cheater. He may, for instance, make dull stereotyped assignments that fail to challenge the student's interest or ability. When written work is not checked, poorly motivated students find it more comfortable to hand in someone else's writing than to make the effort of producing their own (even good writers may lose interest when they sense that they have no "audience"). Caught in a pressure for "higher standards," the teacher may set impossible assignments or judge writing by standards beyond all reasonable achievement. Some teachers by their negative approach may actually create an atmosphere of contest with their students, the object of which is to outwit one another—not to improve writing skills. "We figured Mr. Green sat up nights scheming ways to keep us from cheating, so naturally we all tried to fool him," one student reported. And in the faculty room, Mr. Green was probably saying to his colleagues, "What's wrong with this generation? All they think about is getting out of work. I wouldn't trust one of them!" On the surface of it, the problem seems to lie in part with whom the schools employ to teach, and with the conditions and loads under which the teachers work. But even here, the problem has its roots in the mores and attitudes of our society.

Of all teachers, the teacher of English is in the best position to encourage a respect for honesty in writing—and for honesty in principle, it might be added. Countless testimonials to the decisive influence of a teacher's positive attitude are on record in countless guidance offices. "We just never thought of trying to cheat in Miss Smith's classes," or "Somehow Mr. Brown made us all feel that he trusted us all the way, so naturally no one cheated."

By taking into account the interests and abilities of his students when he makes assignments, by stressing self-improvement instead of grades, and by providing a sincerely interested audience for most pieces of student composition, the teacher can do his share to cut down materially the incidents of plagiarism. In the long run, however, the solution to the problem remains in the hands of our whole society.

6

Books about "how to write," almost without exception, are the works of either frustrated run-of-the-mill or only part-time authors. Though the teacher-author may write about the writing process, the full-time author seldom takes time to. Though the top rank or professional writer may on occasion let slip clues to how he personally writes, he never offers a fool-proof formula. He knows too well the role that individuality plays in his demanding art. He knows that one writer may be content if in a day he manages to turn out 200 words, whereas another in the same length of time may write 2,000. He knows that one writer may stop to polish and revise details as he writes, whereas another sketches in the outlines of his ideas roughly, leaving the revision till another day. One writer can work only with a pencil containing lead of a certain softness; another can compose only on the typewriter. One can collect his thoughts only in the dark of the night, writing from midnight till dawn; another rises at dawn and writes until lunch time. And thus it goes, each writer establishing habits of work that he finds more efficient and congenial than any others.

We suspect that most writers, if they had to, could adapt themselves to a different set of habits, but our point here is the more general one that successful writers do have habits and do practice a systematic approach to their work, whatever it may be. For most writers, these systems grow out of the trial-and-error efforts of their school days. Both teachers and parents would do well, therefore, to encourage children to systematize their writing practices at an early age, though in doing so they should take account of each child's physical, emotional, and mental capacities—and handicaps. Whatever the child grows up to be—novelist, doctor, lawyer, salesman, or housewife holding office in a community club or aid society—the ability to gather, organize, and express ideas in an orderly, rather than a haphazard, way will be of crucial value. However, while urging orderly work habits, the parent or teacher must avoid the danger of putting on pressure in such a way as to stifle the inclination to write. Genius ordinarily finds its own order and is well insulated against any limitation that it finds offensive, but the less gifted can more easily lose spontaneity and willingness to produce if external working conditions are overorganized.

Everyone's life—student's, parent's, teacher's—would be ever so much more comfortably simple if there were a single, definable way to develop writing skill. But this is not the case. Perhaps the old folk saying "There's more than one way to skin a skunk" applies here; perhaps it doesn't. At any rate, here are a few of the more important matters in composition teaching about which there is wide disagreement. College professors and high school teachers with impressive records of successful classroom experience speak both for and against each practice; perhaps, therefore, the only sensible position for a parent to take is that of watchful observer. If your child appears to be learning successfully to write, then whatever system the teacher is using must be right—or at least is doing no harm. On the other hand, the fact that a particular student's writing shows little or no improvement does not necessarily prove that the system is at fault, because many factors are at work—social and sexual drives, economic pressures, environmental influences, academic stimulation. This admittedly is the kind of statement that parents (especially if they are critical of the school) find hard to swallow. Yet in justice to the facts, these factors cannot be casually set aside. They do influence the way a person works—whether in school or out.

THE DAILY THEME VERSUS SPACED
WRITING ASSIGNMENTS

The every-student-write-a-theme-a-day formula originated at Harvard University in 1884. For years Harvard freshmen submitted a composition each day, whether or not they really had anything to say. In time, Harvard abandoned this system, but not before many secondary teachers of English throughout the country had come to regard it as the ideal way to teach writing—though their large class loads prevented most from adopting it.

On paper, the theme-a-day approach to writing makes sense, for theoretically the more often a person practices any skill, the more proficient he should become. Critics of this approach point out, however, that good writing results only when the writer has something that *he* considers important to say—and most people do not have something important to say every day. Most teachers with their over-sized classes, critics point out, cannot possibly read and evaluate a theme a day. Yet without an interested and critical reader, writing is likely to become pointless busywork, because the writer must have a recognizable purpose in what he says. The purpose primarily is (or should be) communication. The student writer who does not visualize his reader, who is writing merely to fulfill the requirements of an assignment, seldom succeeds in communicating anything but his paucity of ideas.

As yet there is no scientific evidence to indicate whether an automatic assignment of this kind produces better results than a thoughtful piece of writing composed at less frequent intervals, though as nearly as can be judged, the majority of teachers today seem to favor the occasional well-thought-out theme, which they have time to read carefully and to comment on.

In antithesis to the theme-a-day philosophy is the "permissive" concept of "write whenever you think you have something to say." Given such an assignment, some children with a built-in instinct for writing manage well enough, but the large majority of students who need more definite direction are lost. So far as we know, no public school today advocates this method, though here and there an individual teacher may practice it on his own. If he is an exceptional teacher, but only so, he may obtain desirable results.

LONG VERSUS SHORT COMPOSITIONS

"Long" and "short" are relative words so that it is never very clear what is meant when either is applied to a piece of writing. "Short," for example, may apply to a single paragraph, to a 300-word paper, or to a novel like Hersey's *A Single Pebble*. Yet in the classroom these words do suggest some practical limitations. To most teachers a short paper probably connotes one that is written "out of the head" with a minimum of planning and outlining, and likely completed within a class period or less. A long paper, on the other hand, is one that requires reading and investigation, that leans on a formal outline. It runs from 500 to 1,000 words or more in length, and it may require days, even weeks, to complete. In college, these are commonly called "term papers."

A topic of frequent debate among composition teachers is the importance of one or the other in the teaching of writing. Despite the argument on the one side that the short theme, even the single paragraph, offers the writer practice in every aspect of good composition, and on the other side, that a short paper cannot possibly develop the ability to plan and carry thought through a sustained piece of writing, the debate seems rather academic.

This is not, after all, an either-or issue. Who can question that students should have practice in writing both long and short papers? How many of each they should be asked to write, however, brings us back to the very practical problem of class size and teacher load. Ideally, in the upper years of high school, a teacher with a daily load of 100 students should ask for at least two long papers of no fewer than 1,000 words each per semester. When these papers are not in process, the teacher should require one short composition of between 100 and 300 words at least every two weeks.

At the junior high school and intermediate level (grades 4 to 6), compositions should naturally be shorter. Teachers of intermediate grades certainly should be able to read a minimum of one-page or page-and-a-half compositions from each child each week—unless, of course, they are saddled with abnormally large classes, which too frequently is the case. Probably most elementary school children write much more at times. Junior high school teachers, especially at the seventh- and eighth-grade levels, should resist the temptation to apply high school standards (particularly unreasonably long composition assignments), just as high school teachers must realize that they are not teaching mature college students.

The amount of writing required, however, should and must vary in terms of the grade level. A third-grader of modest ability, for example, should not be expected to write more than a brief story or paragraph of a few sentences; the precocious primary child can and will write at much greater length. A fair expectation for a sixth-grader might be three or four coherent paragraphs. A ninth-grader should also be able to write three or four coherent paragraphs, but these paragraphs should be much more fully developed than the sixth-grader's. The high school junior may well be asked to write carefully developed themes of 300 to 500 words on extemporaneous subjects, or as many as 1,000 words when he is given adequate time to gather material on his subject. The New York State Regents examination in English for eleventh- and twelfth-graders contains a composition question that requires the writing of a 250- to 300-word composition on any one of about fifteen widely differing topics. The student has approximately one hour to devote to this part of the examination. This examination, however, is designed for students in roughly the upper 50 per cent of ability who are preparing for college.

But length again, as we have noted, is relative. The object in writing is not to turn out a certain number of words to satisfy the teacher's assignment. The aim of all writing should be to say what one has to say; when there is nothing more to say, the writer *should* stop. Too much emphasis on length requirements inevitably produces student writers who waste valuable time on counting words—time that could more profitably be spent on revision. It is common knowledge that one writer may take 500 words to say what another writer can say as well in 100 words. For this reason, some teachers prefer to make composition assignments in terms of number of paragraphs or pages rather than of words. The wisest teacher sets no ironclad, inflexible limit at all.

SUPERVISED VERSUS UNSUPERVISED WRITING

Most teachers prefer to have as much of the composition work done in class as possible for a number of reasons. First, they believe that more can be accomplished by teaching during the actual act of writing than by lecturing about what should or should not be done before and after the fact. They can make certain that conditions surrounding the writing act are as ideal as possible. Most important, if the child is in doubt or has a question regarding the work, he can immediately confer with the teacher.

Perhaps *your* child has perfect conditions under which to write and study at home, but for many children this is not true. Though guidance counselors try their best to keep teachers informed about children with environmental handicaps, with today's spiraling enrollments, their information is only partially complete. A goodly number of students literally have no place in which to do their homework. Living in homes with inadequate space, blaring televisions, lack of facilities (such as desks, good lighting, or ink), and too often surrounded by adults unsympathetic to either the process or the aims of study, far too many able students have no place to do school work once they are outside the school. The plight of reluctant students is even more hopeless, because they lack the will to learn even when study conditions are ideal.

Under such adverse circumstances, a few of the more fortunate may find study space in the neighborhood library or in a friend's home where facilities may be more favorable. (Some cities have volunteer organizations that sponsor and run study halls in public buildings; college or university students monitor these halls for the experience of working with children.) But for many students, these substitutes for good study conditions at home are not available.

Another reason some teachers prefer to supervise personally the writing of their students is one they do not like to discuss publicly. This is the unhappy fact that some students, for one reason or another, fail to understand the moral issue involved in submitting work not their own. It is true that we live in an age of "committee" projects, from which we will never escape (and modern students should be given plenty of practice in committee writing); nevertheless, "copying someone else's report" is *not* good committee procedure. Certainly it is not a way to develop one's skill in written expression. Or one's moral character either!

Worse yet, some parents, having been unduly panicked by the current stress on "high grades" in the race for college entrance, too easily delude themselves into believing it perfectly all right to help their children write better compositions—to the point where teachers are sometimes not sure (though they have strong suspicions) about whose compositions they are reading. (The preceding chapter discussed the general problem of plagiarism. Here the concern is with the more subtle issue of parent-child "collaboration.") You may believe that the teacher should speak out loud and clear against such dishonesty, but the problem is not so easily solved. When absolute proof is lacking, a teacher has to be even more cautious about making accusations than a store detective in picking up a shoplifter. If the teacher doesn't see the parent actually at work, and the possibility of doing so is negligible, how can he do more than make polite and subtle insinuations? Because parents of this kind are obviously lacking in principle, and because children tend to accept and imitate the morality (or lack of it) of the parent, about the only course open to the teacher is to observe the child in the actual process of writing. This is possible, of course, only in the classroom.

Under this system, as in every policing effort, honest students are in some respects penalized. Some children who are able writers find the classroom atmosphere distracting. Others have good conditions at home for study and writing, and parents who understand the purposes of education. But we do not mean to exaggerate the incidence of dishonesty in this connection. Actually, the alert, experienced teacher has little difficulty distinguishing the child who is doing his own work from the child who is not. Insofar as he is able, he provides compensatory opportunities for the sincere student to demonstrate his ability in every way possible, both in and out of class.

THE "WORKED-OVER" COMPOSITION VERSUS
THE "QUICKIE"

Related to the preceding problem is that of the relative value of the quickly written, extemporaneous paper as compared to the formally planned and carefully revised composition. Is the child who can "toss off" a good piece of writing to be considered superior to the one who must have time to mull over and change in some way almost every word and sentence that he writes? Here we might turn to professional writers for a clue. At Fort Ticonderoga Museum are some original manuscripts of Kenneth Roberts' historical novels—thick logbooks in which he has written his novels longhand on the left-hand pages; the right-hand pages, reserved for revisions, are almost completely blank! For a more famous example, we can point to Keats' sonnet "On First Looking into Chapman's Homer," which the poet reportedly delivered to a friend within a few hours of the time that he wrote it. For every one of these examples, though, we can cite writers who agonize over each separate work they write and who take years to complete each piece. In other words, we cannot generalize, for most successful writers are in agreement that their best writing is "one tenth genius and nine tenths sweat."

Again we are not dealing with an either-or issue. Students should have a varied experience—through practice, almost anyone becomes more skillful and facile at saying quickly what lies at the top of his mind. But some people will always need a longer gestation period for their ideas than others. And a good deal of our writing is too important to be dashed off like a note to the milkman. This fact applies as surely to young beginning writers as to mature professionals.

If good writing is basically the product of good thinking, then perhaps the advantage finally lies with those writers who think about and work over their original statements for a considerable time before exposing them to the reader, or in the case of students, to the teacher.

THE WRITING LIFE OF THE ADULT

The major emphasis in composition textbooks is on the practicality of knowing how to write well. But what exactly does this mean? Is it a matter of using the right punctuation? Of accurate spelling? Of choosing the most effective words? Of logical paragraphing? Of sound thinking? Or is it the judicious combination of all these matters, plus others?

We have to be realistic. At certain times, any one of these factors may determine the effectiveness of a given piece of writing. But if we judge by the whole body of writing, both literary and nonliterary, we must quickly concede that the common denominator of all good writing is *clear thinking*. Whether one is writing a letter to the Internal Revenue Service, a sonnet on the power of love, or a recipe for the parish cookbook, honesty, good sense, relevance, and accuracy of thought are most likely to spell success.

What are the main kinds of writing in which adults are likely to engage?

1. *Letter writing.* In their business, social, and personal affairs most adults find letter writing unavoidable. (If especially successful in their work or profession, of course, they may find that dictating to a secretary rather than actual writing is the skill they need!)

2. *Report writing.* In this modern age, clearly written reports are demanded of doctors, politicians, educators, executives, generals, and PTA workers, to mention only a few.

3. *Advertising copy writing.* A growing army of writers are engaged in creating advertising copy for our larger industrial and agricultural producers. Most small businessmen, however, have to write their own advertising copy.

4. *Journalistic writing.* This type of writing ranges from the committee member seeking publicity for the annual church supper to the board of education member trying to get the facts of a bond issue before the public. The number of ordinary citizens who find themselves engaged in writing for press, radio, or television is increasing constantly.

5. *Writing for publication.* Though only a relatively few of those who try to become famous novelists, poets, essayists, or playwrights succeed, the number of people engaged in writing material for the thousands of magazines, books, and other types of publications is rather amazing and increases notably each year. By becoming a social hermit or an anonymous cog in some unimportant machine, a person might possibly live out his life without ever "taking pen in hand." In the face of society's growing complexity, these methods of escape are not as easy to achieve as they once were.

The College Entrance Examination Board, as well as other authoritative voices, maintains that in order to have writing properly taught in our schools, the English teacher must be assigned no more than four classes per day and a total load of not more than twenty-five pupils per class. As matters now stand, the majority of English teachers, being human beings and not martyrs, simply cut down on the number of compositions assigned—or, less frequently, they assign compositions that they make no attempt to read and correct. They do so with regret and with a gnawing sense of frustration. If our society is really concerned about the current state of student writing and genuinely desirous of doing something about it, then here at least is the first step—to create conditions that will enable English teachers to make use of their specialized skill, at least where the teaching of writing is involved.

In honesty it must be pointed out that simply reducing each English teacher's load will not in itself improve the quality of student writing. But with manageable class sizes, the experience gained from reading a greatly increased number of student compositions, plus the time to confer individually with student writers, as well as to use other effective techniques for teaching writing, English teachers should be able to remove many of the causes of public complaint about the quality of student writing today.

STYLE AND THE YOUNG WRITER

7

Almost everyone is affected in one way or another by a writer's style, whether he is reading a sports column, a current best-seller, or even the text of a presidential address. He chuckles over a particular choice of words, or feels the sting of an idea because of an adroitly turned phrase, or experiences a sense of pleasure at what he is reading that is quite divorced from its content. Most readers are aware of style when it is present, though they may not be able to describe technically exactly what it is the writer has done to create it. But recognizing style in the work of others is one thing; developing it in your own writing is quite another.

True individuality and polish even in the style of professionals is the culmination of years of experience and care in writing to express attitudes and feelings as well as thoughts. Some children show evidences of original expression in their very early writings, possibly because of unusual insight, possibly because they have heard and read much vividly written literature. Some teachers believe that boys' and girls' style is the essence of their individuality preserved from early efforts by their having been given many opportunities to write what they think and feel. At any rate, a person achieves genuine style only after he has learned to state his ideas clearly and accurately and has developed a distinct personality that colors and shapes his use of language. Style heightens the effectiveness of anything we say or write, but it is no substitute for basic sense. Though some individuals seem to have been born with an instinct for style, most writers develop it the hard way—by experiment followed by frequent and conscious practice.

Actually, most writers "try on" a number of styles in the course of their development before they arrive finally at the style that marks their mature writing. This is as it should be, for no one maintains a static relationship to life or his fellowmen. Perhaps no profounder observation has even been made on the subject of style than De Buffon's statement, "Style is the man."

Before a teacher begins to worry about matters of style in the writing of his students, he had better make certain that they can express their ideas reasonably well in the common, expected patterns of English, that they have a vocabulary adequate to their basic needs, that they understand the simpler workings of punctuation, and that they have a sense of the importance of structure both in the paragraph and in the whole composition.

But at every stage of the child's development, the teacher should never impose restrictions or offer discouragements to the child who is instinctively searching for a writing style of his own. Often the one or two flashes of originality in handling language that appear occasionally in a child's paper far outweigh such other factors as misspelling, faulty sentences, and the like. It is no exaggeration to say that the greatest threat to any young writer's style is the red pencil in the fist of a determinedly literal teacher!

SENSITIVITY TO LANGUAGE

A large vocabulary may be one indication of a person's intelligence level (or his camera-mindedness), but it is no guarantee that he will be effective as a writer. English is blessed with one of the largest supplies of synonyms of any language in the world. Was last evening's much publicized television spectacle *abominable, corrupting, depraved, evil, immoral, pernicious, vicious, unwholesome, worthless*—or was it merely *bad?* The fact that one child describes it as having been *pernicious* may be impressive, but it may also be inaccurate. The ability to choose the *exact* rather than the "big" word is one sign of a good writer and a sound thinker.

This is not to say that a supply of synonyms is not a useful part of a student's vocabulary. In fact, the more synonyms from which a child has to choose the more accurate his writing will be—if he knows how to make the right choice. To learn to discriminate intelligently among synonyms, a speaker or a writer must understand that words have two kinds of meaning: *denotation* and *connotation.* The denotation of a word is its exact, literal meaning as set down in the dictionary. Connotation is the additional meaning that a word suggests or implies. The synonyms *slender* and *skinny* share the denotation "thin; not fat." The connotation of the former is "attractively or becomingly thin," whereas the latter suggests "unpleasant boniness." In one way or another, most of the more important words that we use carry an extra meaning. Not to be aware of it is to miss a good deal of what is said and written, for the full meaning of a word consists of both its denotation and its connotation.

To the writer who is looking for the best words to express his ideas, this understanding of the two-part meaning of words is especially important. A popular misconception, shared unfortunately by some teachers of English, is that "synonyms are words that mean the same thing." Actually no words ever have exactly the same meaning. They may have the same denotation, but they always differ in connotation. Children should not be urged to use synonyms in their writing merely for the sake of substituting new and unusual words. A good writer chooses one synonym over another because for his purpose it conveys the meaning more exactly.

Most dictionaries take this into consideration in their listing of synonyms. The *Thorndike-Barnhart High School Dictionary,* for example, follows the main entry for *disaster* with this discussion of synonyms:

> SYN. **Disaster, calamity, catastrophe** mean a great misfortune. **Disaster** applies to an event which happens suddenly or unexpectedly, through human fault, mechanical or structural failure, or the forces of nature, and causes much loss and suffering: *The failure of the bank was a disaster for the farmers.* **Calamity** applies to a disaster which causes intense suffering and grief, often to a great number: *The attack on Pearl Harbor was a calamity.* **Catastrophe** suggests a disaster which is final and complete, causing loss that can never be made up: *A modern war is a catastrophe.*[1]

Notice that this discussion begins with a statement of the denotation that these three words share in common, then proceeds to explain their differences in connotation. The younger, inexperienced writer should probably not be held responsible for these distinctions, but the occasion for his using any of them is rather remote. As he progresses in school, however, he is expected not only to add constantly to the number of words he knows but to use more precisely those words already learned. This includes discriminating accurately among available synonyms.

Sensitivity to language is only partly the product of direct teaching. No one can say exactly how much, but it seems rather certain that one of the surest ways to develop a feeling for words is to read good literature. Also important is the language that a child experiences in the home and in other areas of his environment. If he is hostile to his parents, who use *isn't,* but admires some companions who say *ain't,* the chances are he will lean to the use of the latter. Next to motivating a child to read good literature, perhaps the teacher's most important contribution in this area is to awaken the child's interest in language as language. Only when he has been shown the manner in which language works is he likely to pay proper attention to the qualities of the words that he speaks and writes.

Most of the widely used standardized vocabulary tests contain numbers of items that claim to test the student's perceptiveness of verbal connotation as well as the extensiveness of his literal word knowledge. For many years, one third of the English Achievement Test of the College Entrance Examination Board attempted to determine the candidates' sensitivity to the meaning and use of words. Evidence as to how well these testing instruments succeed in their intention is not conclusive.

THE USE OF SLANG

A great deal has been written about and against slang. Viewed in perspective, slang is not the serious threat to our language that many people imagine. The fact is that the creation and use of new and novel language has been a normal activity of man throughout his recorded history, though for some reason the English-speaking people have produced more than their share. Most slang dies a quick and natural death from overwork, but some slang survives to become a colorful and permanent part of the language: *highbrow, rubberneck, pushover, yes-man, honky-tonk, leatherneck, hick, stuffed shirt, holdup.* Though words of this kind are heard mainly in informal, everyday speech, they are not completely unknown to formal English. When a slang word does survive, it is because it expresses a shade of meaning for which we have no other adequate word.

Purists object to slang because, to them, any change in the language, however rational, is a corruption. More thoughtful speakers do not object to slang itself, but to the fact that many young people instead of limiting their use of it to appropriate occasions tend to use it indiscriminately at all times. Instead of bothering to use a precise word, they let an overworked slang word like *swell* or *lousy* express their meaning vaguely on almost any occasion. Thus their vocabularies tend to remain static or even to atrophy, for "Gresham's Law" applies to language as well as to money: "Vague, poorly chosen" words tend to drive "exact" words out of circulation.

Slang is subject to the same usage conventions that affect all other parts of the language. Some slang is found only in the nonstandard

English of uneducated speakers. On the other hand, many a well-educated clergyman, professor, or high government official has found on occasion that a well-chosen slang word serves his purposes well. He may use it for color, for humor, or for emphasis. There is no question, though, that too heavy a reliance on slang produces speech and writing that is trite and flabby. Unless it says something in a way that no other word can, slang is a form of stereotype—an obstruction to exact thinking and communication.

King Canute could not turn back the sea, and parents and teachers would do well not to condemn categorically the use of slang by their children. It appeals especially to the young. A good part of their enjoyment of it can undoubtedly be traced to a combination of their delight both in experimentation and in nonconformity. Perhaps the best attitude for teacher and parent is one of patient acceptance, combined with a continuing demonstration that a person can speak clearly and colorfully without slang.

THE "CORRECT" VERSUS THE EFFECTIVE SENTENCE

The student-written composition in which every sentence is grammatically impeccable is not necessarily the one that a teacher or anyone else delights in reading. Too many students are conditioned to react thoughtlessly to the common signals. Each sentence that they write begins with a subject, is followed by a predicate, and demonstrates no awareness at all of the importance of varying the shape of each sentence to suit or sharpen the thought it expresses—if indeed it has a genuine thought. In the writing of these students, the lack of sentence variety results in a monotonous flow of grammatically identical patterns that blurs even those ideas worthy of consideration. An important source of style, in other words, lies in the writer's ability to mold sentences in such a manner that they unify, relate, emphasize, color the idea—or fragment of an idea—that they attempt to communicate.

In the early stages of writing, when the teacher is the children's secretary and writes down what they dictate, sentences are often quite short, simple, and unconnected, possibly because the teacher leads the way through questioning. For example, note the sentences in this third-grader's story.

> My daddy took me to the zoo. We saw the animals. I liked the monkeys best. They swung by their tails. I threw some peanuts to the monkeys. They grabbed them fast. Some got to quarreling. Daddy and I laughed at them.

However, samples of children's writing in the preceding chapters indicate that many boys and girls write in varied style and not uncommonly in lengthy, quite complicated sentences. Probably when there is considerable exploratory discussion and when children early learn to write down their ideas independently, the rudiments of style are more likely to appear.

Unless seriously retarded, the child as he matures will, however, without direction from the teacher, begin to use some of the more common variations of this simple declarative pattern such as the command or question. "My daddy asks me Johnny do you want to go to the park. We saw many animals. I liked the monkeys best. But daddy says don't get too near that cage."

At this stage, the child is usually unaware of and therefore uninhibited by such sophisticated notions as standard spelling and punctuation. He is thinking on paper, putting his ideas down in the order they occur—and instinctively he follows the sentence patterns that he uses so naturally in speech because he hears them used by the adults around him. Thus, without being told, he will write "the White House" and not "the house white (*la maison blanche*)" as the French child does. The fact that one "white house" requires capital letters and another doesn't will have to be taught him as he learns to discriminate.

This method of imitating his own or the spoken sentence patterns of others works very well as long as the child is dealing with his own experiences or describing simple relations between objects: "Last night the wind blew hard. It shook our house. It blew down our favorite apple tree." But when he reaches the stage of having somewhat abstract ideas to write about, ideas that normally he would have no occasion to express orally, then the problem of fitting the thought to the most effective sentence pattern becomes infinitely difficult. Though there is no clear-cut line, most children discover the abstract world sometime after the sixth or seventh grade. Increasingly from this time their writing is influenced by the more complex sentence patterns that they find in their reading.

At this point the question might well be asked, "If students can learn so much of the business of using sentences on their own, why spend so much time on it in school?" The question is best answered by analogy. Most children learn to swim, often quite effectively, without much formal instruction. Seeing grownups in the water, they jump in, flail their arms and legs in imitation—and find themselves afloat and moving. But they do not become really good swimmers until someone takes the time to instruct them in proper breathing, kicking, and stroking. The wise parent does not let his child move from shallow into deep water without these lessons. Similarly, a student moving from the simpler stages of elementary writing toward the more abstract and exacting demands of the college preparatory, the secretarial, or the technical writing course needs special help in learning to put more complicated ideas into the most suitable sentence patterns. He needs this help even when his everyday spoken use of English is quite satisfactory.

This is not a "textbook," so we will indicate only briefly what this help means. The problem is not one of teaching children to use complex and compound sentences, which they do quite naturally (and sometimes overdo). Rather it is one of making them aware of the importance of *relating* ideas accurately in complex sentences (subordination) and in compound sentences (coordination and/or parallelism). Related to these matters, they need help in learning to shape sentences whose thought is more clearly and powerfully expressed through the use of contrast, balance, climax, rhythm, variety, and the like.

In their concern for the individual sentences in student writing, teachers sometimes lose sight of the importance of the whole composition. A dented fender may hurt the owner's sense of pride, but it does not interfere with the functioning of his car. A composition should not be judged mainly by the occasional faulty sentences or misused words it contains, but by its total effect on the reader. The principles of unity, coherence, and emphasis, discovered long ago by the Greeks, operate as much in writing today as they ever did. But still fundamental is the content, or ideas, that the writer is communicating.

Any piece of writing, whether a paragraph, a poem, a research report, or a novel, should be designed to give the reader a sense of its completeness. From the time that a child first begins to write, he needs to be reminded of the simple tripartite elements of unity—the beginning (introduction), the body (development), and the ending (conclusion). This basic design holds for any composition. Within this design, each sentence should relate clearly to the main idea and purpose of the composition, as well as to the section in which it stands.

Writing should be coherent. That is, each sentence should relate unmistakably to those that come before and those that follow it. The young writer should be shown how to recognize and remove unrelated sentences. Also important to coherence is the accurate use of connecting elements such as conjunctions, prepositions, and key words.

Emphasis is the matter of "putting first things first," of making important ideas stand out at the same time that the writer subordinates those of lesser importance. Emphasis may result from the amount of space devoted to an idea, to its location in the total composition, to the words used, or to the sentence patterns employed.

To the degree that any one of these elements—unity, coherence, emphasis—is missing, the composition suffers. Misspellings, run-on and fragmentary sentences, inept punctuation—these faults annoy and momentarily confuse a reader and are regrettable. But when a piece of writing leads you to conflicting conclusions, when it puzzles you with irrelevant statements, or when it does not clearly distinguish the important from the less important ideas for you, then the writer is in serious trouble. Nine times out of ten, the cause is not inability but the student's failure to think about and plan the general outlines of his composition before beginning to write.

FIGURATIVE LANGUAGE

Figures of speech are so common a part of our everyday speech that most of us are not aware how much we depend upon them to make ourselves clear and interesting. For slang, advertising, and informal conversation depend just as heavily upon figurative language as do poetry and other kinds of literature. Our everyday language, in fact, is filled with "dead" figures of speech—figures used so commonly over a long period of time that they have ceased to be recognized as such: the *eye* of a needle, the *head* of the house, the *heart* of the matter, the *face* of the clock, the *foot* of the class, to mention only a few of the thousands that people use daily.

Colloquial usage and slang lean heavily upon figurative language: a *cool cat,* a *drip,* a *hot dog,* a *blockhead.* And literature, of course, could not exist without its vivid and informative figures: *My mind to me a kingdom is, His silver skin laced with his golden blood, The moon is a ghostly galleon tossed upon cloudy seas.* Between these two extremes, the educated speaker or writer makes continuing and effective use of figurative language.

From this, you may rightly conclude that a child does not have to know the technical labels of the various figures of speech in order to use them successfully. There are, after all, almost two hundred different figures, though most are used but rarely. On the other hand, is there any good reason why a high school junior or senior who is preparing for college should not be able to identify some of the more frequently used figures: metaphor, simile, personification, metonomy, synechdoche, hyperbole, and understatement, for example?

Unfortunately, the traditional method of acquainting students with figurative language has been the "metaphor hunt" and "memorization of definitions." Through the years, assignments such as "For tomorrow locate ten metaphors and five similes" have probably caused more children to "hate" the *Odyssey* and other innocent but richly rewarding literary selections than any other single teaching device. Worse yet, they have given generations of students the misconception that figures of speech are "ornaments" with which clever authors decorate their writing.

Nothing could be further from the fact, of course. The fresh, pointed figure of speech is indispensable—at the same time that it adds color to writing, it suggests a shade or facet of meaning that could not be expressed in any other way. Your child's ability to express his thoughts in literal language is basic; if he is going far as a writer, he will have to learn to express the depths and nuances of his mind in figurative language.

Students use figurative language quite naturally in their everyday conversation, but most find it difficult to write. Either they rely on stale, overworked figures (*raining cats and dogs, blanket of snow, eyes sparkling like diamonds*) or they create tortured figures that are colorful enough but do not help communicate their meaning (*on her finger a huge ice cube in a golden halo, a voice as hoarse as a drunken duck's*). But the inexperienced writer must start somewhere. At whichever extreme he begins, he should receive not frustrating criticism but positive help in his efforts to use figurative language that is fresh, vivid, and appropriate to his ideas.

AWKWARDNESS IN WRITING

A young writer often gets into trouble by putting sentence parts together in an uncustomary way or by using more words or grammatical constructions than he needs. His teacher, faced with an impossible number of papers to correct, often can do no more than put the symbol *Awk* in the margin (meaning "an awkward construction," but explaining nothing about the cause of the awkwardness).

Unfortunately the students whose writings contain an excessive number of such flaws are usually the ones who cannot diagnose the causes for themselves. When they see *Awk* in the margin, they understand that something is amiss, but they do not know what. If the teacher is experienced enough or has been provided with time for personal conferences, the exact nature of such errors can be dealt with successfully. If the teacher is unable to pinpoint the cause of the trouble, the child may continue to be an awkward writer for the rest of his life.

Children of native speakers of English are not as likely to mix up their sentence parts as are those with a foreign-language background. For example, a native American child would not be likely to speak or write such an early Zsa Zsa Gabor type of inversion as "Him I should shoot." This kind of awkwardness is understandable in view of the grammatical differences that exist among languages, but it is not entirely excusable. Both native-born children and those with a foreign-language background have their chief difficulty with the placement of modifiers and the accurate use of personal pronouns.

Misplaced modifiers that do not make immediately clear the idea that they modify are common in student writing: "Everyone was astounded at the view coming down the mountain"; or, "Crumpling his fender, he misjudged his distance as he backed into the parking space." The student who is aware of his tendency to misplace modifiers and who carefully rereads what he has written rearranges his sentences to read accurately: "Coming down the mountain, everyone was astounded at the view"; or "Misjudging his distance as he backed into the parking space, he crumpled his fender." Sometimes a modifier has nothing that it can sensibly modify: "After standing in line for an hour, the tickets were all sold." This is easily altered by supplying the proper subject: "After standing in line for an hour, we found the tickets had all been sold." At other times, a modifier seems to make sense in two ways. Does the student who writes "I knew before I arrived the place would be empty" mean that "he knew" before he got there or that it was empty "before" he got there? A simple revision can make the intended meaning clear.

Language purists make a great to-do about the "split infinitive." (A modifier standing between the *to* and the *verb,* as in "to gracefully swoop.") Actually, the split infinitive is a fault only when it sounds awkward and thus distracts attention from its meaning. A critic might justifiably question such a statement as "She told him to slowly and carefully fill the tank," rightfully preferring "She told him to fill the tank slowly and carefully." Not to split the infinitive in a statement such as "He should be warned to carefully avoid overeating" is to misinform the reader. He is not "warned carefully" nor is he advised to "overeat carefully"!

A different kind of awkwardness results from interrupting the normal flow of a sentence unnecessarily: "He ordered, with onions, after they had finally found seats at the counter, hamburgers for two," should sensibly be rearranged to read, "After they had finally found seats at the counter, he ordered hamburgers with onions for two."

Perhaps the most common error of all is the "shifted construction." This occurs, most often in telling a story, when the student fails to indicate ideas that are equally important to the meaning. Instead of writing "Milk is satisfying, flavorful, and nutritious," he slips in his final idea from a modifier to a noun, "Milk is satisfying, flavorful, and a nutritious drink." Shifts of this kind may occur in a number of predictable ways—from one tense to another, from singular to plural forms and vice versa, from single noun to a clause, and the like. Such shifts do not completely distort the meaning, but they lead to awkwardness, and awkwardness confuses the reader.

BACK TO STYLE

If some of the matters covered in this chapter seem unnecessarily detailed, it is because style in writing is the product of many ingredients. These ingredients range from the way a writer chooses and puts his words together to the way he looks at life. Each makes its contribution, and none can be overlooked by the student who wants someday to be considered an educated adult writer.

MARKING AND GRADING

8

Dad's and Mom's blood pressure never rises higher or more surely than when they believe that teacher has not given their Johnny the mark he deserves. Of course, the "grade he deserves" is always a higher grade. Understandably, few if any parents ever raise the objection that the quality of their child's work has been overestimated!

Though this kind of disagreement can occur in any school subject, nowhere is it more likely than in written composition, for even learned professors have been known to offer sharply differing opinions as to the worth of a particular piece of student writing. Subjects like mathematics and history that deal mainly with facts and figures offer much less ground for argument. Composition, which combines the writer's ideas and judgments with his subjective choice of words, sentence patterns, and paragraph division, is quite a different matter, and one that defies "exact" measurement. This is not to say, however, that its "relative" worth cannot be agreed upon.

Mistakenly or not, in the eyes of most parents the grade a child receives is the only proof of the pudding. Many schools try, but few find it really possible or practicable to have you, the parent, sit down face to face with your child's teacher to discuss his work. Even in less crowded schools that provide such conferences, their value is open to question. There is just so much time in the school day—and the time spent talking with you (and a hundred other parents) is time taken away from teaching your child.

These are a few of the reasons it is important for you, as an interested parent, to understand some of the problems the teacher faces in correcting and grading your child's compositions.

If you are inclined not to believe this, try your hand at evaluating these compositions written by fourth-grade pupils upon their return to school from a Thanksgiving recess. Assign each one a grade— *A* for excellent, *B* for good, *C* for average, *D* for poor, *F* for failure.

Paper 1

One Thanksgiving Day the turkey that I ate was as big as an Rhinoceros. It almost took up the whole table. When we finished there was still enough turkey to last us, all seventeen of us, another year. By the time we finished turkey two or three hours had passed. The turkey we had just eaten was probably the biggest one that ever lived on this world. That Thanksgiving, I think, will always be the best one I've had and will have.

Paper 2

On Thanksgiving we went to our country place and we had to get settled down. The next day I went to the road, and I made mud cakes across the road. I put on my army suit and the cars on the road stopped when they saw the mud cakes.

Paper 3

On Thanksgiving I ate my Thanksgiving turkey.
On Friday I went to the planetarium.
On Saturday I did not do anything at all.
On Sunday, I went to the park. I took a buggy ride in the park.

Paper 4

My Thanksgiving is a wonderful day for me. We gave thanks for the day. We had for dinner: turkey, cranberry sauce, nuts, corn, bread. We turned out the light and some candles and said our thanks. My mother and father and my brother too gathered around the fireplace and sang very pretty songs. What did you do on Thanksgiving?

Paper 5

On Thanksgiving Day, I went to the Macy Parade. I sat in the grandstands of Macy with Mama, Grandpappy, and Sister Linda.
Thanksgiving evening Bob Searles, a friend of Mama's came to dinner.
My Sister Linda, lost her favorite dog (a stuffed animal) just before Bob came. We all (except Mommy who was fixing dinner) looked for it but couldn't find it.
After we sat down Linda came running WITH HER DOG and said, "Look I found it on my bed."

Having read these compositions, are you willing to say that one is worth an *A*, whereas another is worth only a *C*? Or that some are "passing," whereas others are "failing"? Or did you perhaps think they are all rather good and deserving of "high" marks? If this is the case, are they all deserving of equally "high" marks? If they are not, which composition would you give *A minus* and which *B plus*? Are you a bit confused at this point? Imagine yourself a teacher with 150 such decisions to make each time that you give a writing assignment!

It is possible and indeed probable that a teacher can and will evaluate in a much more fruitful way than by giving marks like *A* or

B. He is likely to make use of check lists which the students have helped to devise as they have learned one standard after another, then use this standard as a point in their accumulating check lists. For instance, the standards for writing a well-organized, clearly expressed outline might make up a check list like the following:

	Yes	No
Does my paragraph deal with a single topic?		
Does each sentence relate to this topic?		
Are the sentences in the proper order?		
Is each sentence clear?		
Do the sentences begin in different ways?		
(and so on)		

On the basis of such standards, the teacher is likely to write comments on each paper that indicate success in following a particular standard or need for improving the paragraph in the light of another standard. Such comments are evaluative in a constructive and meaningful way. They say helpful things a *B* or *C* cannot possibly say.

WHAT DOES THE MARK ON A COMPOSITION MEAN?

"Aye, there's the rub!" The mark given a particular composition by a teacher at a particular time may mean any one of a score of different things. Perhaps on this assignment the teacher is concerned chiefly with some such relatively minor matter as spelling or punctuation. Or perhaps he is looking at your child's ability to paragraph and organize ideas. Or maybe in assigning this paper he has suggested the use of figurative or affective language. He may (and we hope this is the case) have been mainly interested in the significance and coherence of thought demonstrated by the writer.

Whatever the teacher's concern, it is clear that the mark on a particular composition is meaningful only to the extent that we understand what the teacher is looking for in "today's assignment." If the teacher does not make clear in the assignment what he expects of the writer, what is the student to assume? If the parent does not know the teacher's objective, how can he interpret the grade on the composition his child brings home?

Perhaps here we should clear up a rather important point. Teachers do not read and grade student compositions for the edification of the parents. The one purpose of this time-consuming activity on the teacher's part is, or should be, to help students to write better. The grade on your child's composition may mean one of several things to him. It may serve to tell him how his writing at the moment compares with other writing he has done. It may tell him how his writing compares, in content or in skill, with that of his classmates. It may say that he has not given sufficient thought to his writing or commend him for the excellence of his ideas. The grade together with the teacher's specific comments should tell him what he has done well or not done well enough. But if your child is not interested in improving his writing, the teacher's time and energy have been wasted. Your interest in your child's marks is commendable, but about the only realistic way for you to influence them for the better is to help the teacher make your child more enthusiastic about the act of writing. Scolding and nagging about poor "marks" are likely to have quite the opposite effect.

Most experienced and successful teachers of composition are more likely to regard grades as a necessary nuisance than as motivation for improvement. They are more concerned with developing in each child a sense of *self*-criticism. They want the child to recognize that writing, though seldom a pleasure, can result in great personal satisfaction. To this end, they rely chiefly on specific comments, written marginally or passed directly along in a student-teacher conference. They mark or correct only the most flagrant technical errors; they give the bulk of their attention to the content of the writing.

Much student writing is inane and pointless because the student is not writing for a real and interested audience, but for the "teacher" and his "red pencil." The experienced composition teacher does everything possible, therefore, to substitute for this teacher-audience image a sense of writing for a "reader who cares." When he reads and grades his students' writing, this teacher carefully puts aside his own opinions and prejudices. He tries to judge the writing in the light of the writer's purpose as well as its effect on the audience whom the child is addressing. At the elementary level, the teacher often reads the pupils' paragraphs and stories to the class. The writer, as well as his classmates, notes the effective or ineffective features of the written product (how interesting is the theme and general treatment, how well organized, whether sentences vary in pattern and their beginnings, whether there are sentence fragments and run-on sentences). In teaching each child to evaluate his own product and make revisions before submitting his paper, the teacher encourages him to read it aloud to himself (in a subdued whisper, we trust!). Oral reading is probably the surest check on sentence structure because a poorly constructed sentence seldom "sounds right" when heard.

After a child's paragraph or story has been read aloud, it may sometimes be discussed in the light of the standards he had in mind as he wrote. His classmates should be encouraged to look for and comment on strong points first, and occasionally they may suggest an important way to improve the child's written product. This "helpful" type of suggestion should involve a standard for which many of his classmates need to work; the teacher makes clear that each member of the class should strive in the next paper to achieve this standard, and he makes clear how to go about it. Valuable as well-led class discussion may be in evaluating a pupil's writing, the teacher does not forget how important his experienced criticism and guidance are in promoting improvement in writing. His conference with a pupil, his timely suggestions as the child checks his own paper before submitting it, are essential.

WRITING WITH A PURPOSE

Your child writes best when he understands why he is writing. Sometimes this reason is furnished by the teacher when he asks for an informative report, an entertaining story, a vivid description, a convincing argument. A more desirable situation is one in which the student determines his own purpose for writing. He knows what he wants to say, and why. His purpose is thus simplified to the matter of saying what he has to say in the most effective way possible. Whether suggested by someone else or originating in the student, the ideas communicated are the main concern of writing. There is no point in relaying them, however, if they are not expressed in clear, accurate, and lively English.

Still, many subjective elements may interfere with a teacher's judgment when he reads a composition. To offset this tendency toward bias, a teacher must have in mind some standards against which to measure different aspects of writing and the work of different writers. Experienced teachers have generally evolved such standards from experience. For young teachers (and for interested parents) a number of possibly helpful suggestions are available.

The National Council of Teachers of English, for example, publishes special theme paper (called Ideaform Paper) for schools to issue to their students for formal compositions. On each sheet of Ideaform paper the student is reminded of this set of standards to guide him in his writing:[1]

---

[1] Copyright 1955 by the National Council of Teachers of English and used by permission.

Comments on the ideas, or content:

Evaluation of the form

	Good	Fair	Poor
Organization			
Development			
Sincerity of purpose and expression			
Sentence structure and punctuation			
Paragraphing			
Usage			
Choice of words			
Spelling			
Penmanship and general appearance			

Other comments:

Arno Jewett, former director of the National Education Association's Dean Langmuir English Composition Project and also Language Arts Specialist in the United States Office of Education, offered these "points to consider in correcting themes" as part of his report on the project:

1. *Purpose*
   a. How clearly is the purpose or thesis stated?
   b. How well is it achieved?
   c. Is the topic sufficiently limited?
2. *Content*
   a. Are the main ideas evident to the reader?
   b. Are details given to develop main ideas or topics?
   c. Are examples used to illustrate and support general statements?
   d. Is the content related to the writer's purpose?
   e. Are the facts or evidence accurate or verifiable?
3. *Organization* (Unity)
   a. Does the introduction prepare the reader for what follows?
   b. Is there a clear relationship among main ideas?
   c. Are transitions from one idea or topic to another clearly made?
   d. Does the theme have a definite, satisfactory conclusion?
4. *Style* (Flavor)
   a. Is sentence structure varied and smooth?
   b. Is diction vivid and suitable?
   c. Is figurative language fresh and fitting?
   d. Is the tone appropriate to purpose and subject?
   e. Does the theme hold the reader's attention?
5. *Mechanics*
   a. Have the conventions of grammar and usage been observed?
   b. Is correct punctuation used to aid the reader?
   c. Are words spelled correctly?[2]

[2] Arno Jewett and Charles E. Bish (eds.), *Improving English Composition* (Washington, D.C.: National Education Association, 1965), pp. 95–96. Used by permission of the National Education Association.

These standards, of course, must be applied in varying and appropriate degree. A high school senior, for instance, may reasonably be expected to show more skill in using metaphors and commas than a ninth-grader. In lower grades where the spontaneous expression of ideas is of first importance, standards such as these have no place at all.

A book widely used in courses training future English teachers (*Teaching Language and Literature,* by Loban, Ryan, and Squire) sums up the problem nicely in a section entitled "Clarifying Purposes of Correction":

> The teachers' purpose is not so much to improve a particular composition as to help pupils to become more self-critical and to improve their writing ability. Thus he needs to ask himself whether or not his correction procedures are effective. For example, the careful and meticulous marking of every error has been rejected by almost everyone who has studied the problem. One study of compositions corrected by teachers of college freshmen showed that only twenty per cent of the comments helped the writer become more self-directive, and almost thirty-six per cent of the comments were worthless or positively false. Such findings show a lack of standards or critical wisdom on the part of many who read compositions. In another study the weekly themes of two groups of ninth grade students were read and checked in two different ways. For the first group, themes were read by means of an error guide and code. All errors were checked and the themes were assigned grades. They were then returned to the pupils to be rewritten and returned to the teacher in corrected form. For the other group, writing just as frequently, only a grade was given. No errors were checked or indicated in any manner and no rewriting of corrected themes was required. Comparison of the relative improvements of these pupils showed that although the detailed theme correction was slightly more effective in eliminating technical errors, the difference was not great enough to justify such a tremendous expenditure of teacher time.[3]

LETTERS OR NUMBERS?

Numerical grades on compositions give an illusion of exactness and are therefore more satisfying to the pupil or parent who is intent on "beating out" classmates. Experienced teachers invariably prefer to give a letter grade because they very well know the impossibility of any one reader's arriving at a mathematically exact and fair judgment of a particular piece of writing, whether Shakespeare's or some unknown student's.

[3] Walter Loban, Margaret Ryan, and James R. Squire, *Teaching Language and Literature* (New York: Harcourt, Brace & World, Inc., 1961), p. 503.

Paul Diederich, of the Educational Testing Service, writing in the "Notes on Grading Essays for Writing Ability" issue of *The English Record,* amusingly but pointedly underlined the issue by suggesting the use of only three grades in evaluating student compositions—*A, C,* and *F.* Those papers that in one way or another interest and excite the reader even as they inform him, he would award an *A.* To papers that are dull, but still not a disgrace to the school technically, he would assign a *C.* But papers that are clearly a disgrace to the school, both in content and in form—that, in his colorfully uninhibited language, give the reader the impression that he has "passed through the bowels of the intellect"—he would give an *F* and try to forget![4]

Most teachers would agree with this basic assumption but would probably argue for somewhat more flexibility—an *A-B-C-D-F* scale or perhaps even a 1 to 10 rating scale. Almost none would support the accuracy or realism of a 0 to 100 scale applied to student written compositions. For as we have noted earlier, who can say honestly that one composition is worth exactly 64 credits and another is worth 65?

DOUBLE GRADES

Not uncommonly a student has interesting ideas, a fresh outlook on the world about us, but shows little or no concern in his writing about such matters as spelling, punctuation, or paragraphing. Some students, on the other hand, have dull, threadbare, insignificant ideas, yet manage to express them in grammatically impeccable English. Which is worth more?

Unwilling to fail a student on either technique or form alone, some teachers resort to a double grade. That is, for the same paper, a student may receive an *A* for content and a *D* for technique. Most teachers, however, apparently feel that this method begs the question. They prefer to judge the composition as a whole, placing most weight upon what the student has to say, but deducting credit when mechanical errors confuse the sense or otherwise detract from the effect he is trying to achieve. Double grades are difficult to convert into "averages," and from the student writer's viewpoint confusing and an open invitation to rationalization. Unless he has an unusually strong ambition to improve, he is likely to rest content with the higher of the two grades, whichever it is.

---

[4] Paul Diederich, *What's It Worth?* Abstract from "Notes on Grading Essays for Writing Ability," *The English Record,* **IV**:2 (Winter 1954), published at Colgate University for the New York State English Council.

THEN AND NOW

Lest some parents and teachers think that we are underwriting a "permissive" approach to the grading of composition, we go back more than half a century to an essay on the subject, written in 1912 by one of the most respected composition textbook authors and English teachers of the time, Alfred M. Hitchcock. Together with a number of other suggestions, he says:

> *Don't be a ferret.* Overlook many errors. Take it for granted that some blunders are but marks of youthfulness; let them alone and they will disappear in time. And don't try to make a purse out of a whistle. Some young people haven't much to say and never will have. If a boy has a commonplace mind—or worse, he ought to produce commonplace themes—or worse; and if he has expressed himself within 10 per cent of his maximum of intelligence I am not sure but he should receive ninety even though his compositions, on an absolute scale, merit but twenty or thirty. This rule does not hold in mathematics, nor in Latin, nor in the teaching of literature, perhaps; I believe it does hold in the teaching of composition, where the instructor's sole duty is to train the pupil that he will be able to express himself, regardless of whether that self be a Milton or a Mollusk.[5]

Our intention here is not to champion the "good old days" as such, but to suggest that thinking people in every age seem to share basic agreements about the nature of student writing.

Unhappily, though letter grades are clearly the more realistic answer to the needs of the composition teacher, tradition in most schools requires a numerical rating in every subject—in order to establish an "overall average," whatever that means. The wise teacher nevertheless sticks to his guns where composition is involved, transposing as he must letter grades to numerical grades: commonly, *C minus* = 65; *C* = 70; *C+* = 75; *B minus* = 80; *B* = 85; *B+* = 90; *A* = 95; *A+* = ? Teachers may differ slightly in their interpretations, but in general this is the scale.

TEACHER'S PERSONAL COMMENT AND/OR A GRADE

The suggestion has several times been made that a teacher's personal comment is more meaningful and helpful to the student than underlinings, correction symbols, and grades. A student writer—any writer—does not take kindly to passive reading and cold, precise "correction." He likes to feel that what he has written has made an

[5] Alfred M. Hitchcock, "A Composition on Red Ink," *English Journal,* **I** (May 1912), 76.

impression. He would prefer, of course, a positive impression, but even a negative comment that shows that his teacher is interested in his ideas is welcome.

In this respect, the number of papers to be corrected presents the conscientious teacher with a real problem. Merely to say "Good" or "Your writing has improved" is not enough. The student writer is helped only if the teacher's comments are both encouraging and specific. The best comment may be a question: "Is this a sentence?" "Do you really mean 'superior'?" "Good, but what is your point here?" Such comments lead the writer to examine what he has said and to give direction to whatever revisions he decides to make.

A legible handwriting, we might add parenthetically, is essential to clear communication. Not all teachers, unfortunately, recognize this elementary fact. If the teacher's notation or comment is hastily scribbled, a half-hearted student may understandably pass it over— just as an irritated adult reader might. Comments and corrections that go unheeded are a waste of valuable teacher time and effort.

CLASS SIZE AND STUDENT WRITING

All of the matters discussed thus far in connection with the correction and grading of student writing have meaning only when students are given the chance to write. It is no secret that in many schools the large class loads assigned to teachers make the effective teaching of writing all but impossible. The current public concern about the quality of student writing has led here and there, in more enlightened school systems, to the realistic reduction of the English teacher's load. But, on the average, high school and junior high school English classes still range well past the point of diminishing returns. A daily schedule of five classes with a total daily load of 150 students is all too common. Some schools report, as normal, loads of 180 pupils daily per teacher. At the elementary level, where the teaching of the basic skills begins, the picture is no brighter; classes of 50 pupils are not uncommon.

The impact of such unwieldy classes on the amount of student writing and upon the reading and correction of what little may be written seems too evident to need comment. Most critics of the schools, even while they are deploring the quality of student writing and clamoring for improvement, acknowledge this obstacle. Yet even though its seriousness is recognized, most school boards find it more convenient to pass resolutions calling for more and better composition teaching than to hire enough teachers to make the job humanly possible. We often know what we want in our society, but unless it falls under some such category as wine, women, or song, we aren't always willing to pay for it. Though in some of our substandard urban schools the rats are more comfortably housed than our children, a modern Pied Piper would still probably find himself on the list of the unemployed.

The colleges, particularly affected by the poor quality of student writing, have adopted a variety of attitudes to the problem. A few have washed their hands of all responsibility for improving the situation; more, fortunately, are experimenting with a variety of promising programs for upgrading student composition. A good many, in fact, having now shared the problem, are beginning to show some recognition of and sympathy for the plight of the overburdened, often undertrained, high school English teacher. In a new freshman program at a high ranking private eastern men's college, according to a recent report in *The New York Times,* writing and literature will be taught seminar fashion with *no more than ten* students in each section. The chairman of the English department of the college is quoted as saying that the faculty believe writing is like piano playing—taught best to one student at a time. They hope to come as close to this idea as time and budget will permit. Such an ideal situation would be beyond the realm of possibility in most public schools and universities with their burgeoning enrollments, budgetary restrictions, and shortages of trained teachers. But it does point in a sensible direction.

As a practical goal for the high school, James B. Conant, in *The American High School Today,* recommends that English teachers be assigned a daily teaching load of no more than 100 pupils.[6] A teacher with this load, he believes, can reasonably be expected to assign, read, and return one composition per pupil each week. Even with this reduced load, a teacher who assigns a 300-word paper will receive each week a total of about 30,000 words of writing to read, weigh, and (it is hoped) comment on. If he devotes a minimum of five to ten minutes to each paper, he will have to spend between eight and sixteen hours on this activity alone. But since he is released from one teaching period each day to read papers, the amount of extra night work might amount to no more than four to twelve hours per week. This is not, perhaps, an exorbitant demand, but it is a good many hours more than teachers of other subjects are likely to expend. It suggests that anyone entering the teaching profession with the idea of implementing his salary by "moonlighting" had better consider some other field than English!

[6] James B. Conant, *The American High School Today* (New York: McGraw-Hill Book Company, 1959), p. 51.

When we talk about an English teacher with a 100-pupil load, however, we are talking about an almost ideal and as yet largely nonexistent condition. At a generous estimate, probably no more than one in 500 schools comes close to this goal, though the number is slowly increasing. What is the picture when a teacher has five or even six classes daily in which he meets from 150 to 180 pupils? Each 300-word composition assigned will net him 45,000 or more words to read and evaluate—the equivalent of almost half an average length novel. Five minutes given to each paper will require a minimum of twelve hours of night work, or more than two hours of each working day—and this *in addition to* the time that must be given to lesson planning, extracurricular activities, and the other nonteaching duties of which few teachers are free.

Furthermore, with this number of pupils to care for, a two-minute classroom conference (which is actually not long enough to be of much value) with each student to discuss his composition would require more than seven additional hours. To accomplish this, two class periods of each week's five would have to be devoted to this activity alone—clearly an impracticable plan. These real and incontrovertible figures may help to explain why most teachers find it necessary to omit conferring with individual students about their writing, even though such an activity is an important adjunct to the successful teaching of composition.

EXPERIMENTAL ALTERNATIVES

In an effort to find a workable solution to the problem of providing students with adequate practice in writing, a number of schools are experimenting with such assistance as lay readers, closed television projects, master teachers, and large group-small group instruction. Because the latter three devices call for a radical reorganization of the traditional system of scheduling and staffing that most schools are either unwilling or unable to make (not to mention special facilities, which most schools do not have and feel they can not afford), they have been tried out fully in only a few scattered schools.

Because it is costly to produce and maintain and complex to coordinate programs with rigidly scheduled classes, closed circuit television has made little progress. The use of master teachers and large group instruction has had a somewhat wider trial. Under this plan, several hundred tenth-graders, for example, would come together to hear a master teacher lecture on the writing of paragraphs. Theoretically, this would be a "super" lesson, replete with audiovisual aids, that the average teacher would have neither the time nor skill to prepare. The students would then return to their "small" classes where they would put the information received into practice. The chief weaknesses in this device, where composition is concerned, seems to be the element of regimentation required, the ineffectiveness generally of "talking about" writing, and the amount of complicated scheduling that is involved. With more experience, some of these problems may be resolved. But for smaller schools the device will never be entirely practicable.

Of rather more widespread interest is the practice of hiring housewives with college training as theme readers (or, as they are often called, lay readers). The purpose is to relieve English teachers of some of their paper work by having college educated members of a community, often former teachers, take over the work of reading student papers in detail. The readers are trained, are in contact with the teacher whose pupils they serve, and in some cases actually engage in follow-up conferences with the student-writers. A certain proportion of the compositions are read by the teacher, so that he can keep track of the pupil's progress and at the same time check on the work of the lay reader.

Reports on the efficiency of this practice have been mixed. It has, of course, some obvious advantages: more student papers are written and read critically, the reading is more objective, the teacher theoretically has more time for teaching, and apparently there are willing and able people interested in participating. On the other hand, the disadvantages are not easy to overcome. To begin with, the device is cumbersome. It requires expansion of the administrative staff. The teacher has the added burden of briefing his reader. The turnover in readers is likely to be large as the result of such ordinary events as husband's vacations, job transfers, housewife's fatigue, and home responsibilities. Because the successful teaching of writing most usually results from a close personal relationship between teacher and student, the teacher in this plan tends to know relatively less about his students than if he were fully responsible (though this may well be compensated for in the greater amount of writing practice). Finally, the success of the plan rests heavily on a good working relationship between teacher and lay reader. English teachers tend notably to be individualists, and this presents a not unimportant problem. For whatever it is worth, a recent study of the lay reader plan reports that more schools each year are abandoning the device than are adopting it.

Parents who are dissatisfied with the grades on their children's compositions (or with the writing itself!) should keep these facts and figures in mind. And they should not forget that, important as composition is, it is only one of the English teacher's many responsibilities. For he must also teach reading, usage, grammar, speech, and most important of all, literary appreciation, to his 100 to 180 pupils per day. If he is lucky, he will have in addition only an attendance register to keep, a senior play to direct, and an assortment of odd jobs like study hall supervision, magazine fund drive, chaperoning the junior prom, and lunchroom supervision to perform—all important and necessary, but all thieves of the time and energy that should be going into his primary job of teaching! If he is unlucky, he may also be drafted to coach the football team or direct the band, though these irrelevancies are happily becoming less frequently the rule.

TESTS OF WRITING AND
THE WRITING OF TESTS

9

The number of books on the subject of testing that have been pub-lished during the past few years is evidence enough of its growing importance in the modern school. Of course, schools in the past had tests, too, but they were regarded as part of the teaching process. They were the teacher's way of finding out how much his charges had learned, and at the same time they were a "big stick" that helped force students to study. For the most part, they were written by the individual teacher and administered to his own classes.

Today "testing," like so many other things, has become a special-ized field. Testing is still used by teachers to find out how much their students have learned and a few still regard it as a useful threat. But the most important tests that your child may face will be written not by his teacher but by a committee of experts of whom neither you nor he has ever heard. And the test will be given not just to your child in his own school but to thousands of other students in all parts of the country, against whose abilities his will be measured. This will be true in most of the subjects he studies, but it will be particularly true in that area of study that we call "English."

This change in the nature of testing has had both good and bad effects. A committee of experts has greater resources of knowledge and experience to call upon when they write a test than has a single, overworked teacher. On the other hand, the experts can never know with certainty what teachers in individual schools all over the country have been teaching. As he should, each teacher will select materials and give emphasis in a somewhat different way from other teachers. If the teacher's approach differs radically from the testmakers', then his students may well find themselves at a disadvantage. Yet, in spite of this, the teacher may be doing an excellent job of teaching and the test may be a very good test.

No matter what is done to prevent it, as a test achieves state or national importance, it tends to take on a supervisory function. That is, it tends to force teachers to teach *for* the test, regardless of the needs of his particular students and the community. At the same time, it may force other, not as well-prepared, teachers to pay attention to important matters that otherwise they would neglect.

Other possibilities could be explored here, but the point seems clear enough. Testing in the modern school is no longer simply a matter of "checking up" on your child's efforts or of enforcing his attention. It has taken on other, more complex, functions. And nowhere are these functions more difficult to pin down than in a discussion of the evaluation of good writing, more formally called "composition."

Whatever you as a parent may think of tests and their influence upon your child, you might as well accept the idea that they are here to stay, and that the child who cannot survive the rigors of modern testing is severely handicapped in our competitive society. This is not to express unqualified approval of this state of human affairs, but merely to note a fact. From the time he enters school until he is graduated, the modern student is bombarded with a variety of tests. On the basis of his test results, he is diagnosed, measured, placed, selected, grouped, rejected—and on occasion, even rewarded!

Because an understanding of our language and skill in using it are essential to the mastery of all subjects (with the possible exception of mathematics), your child's ability to express himself competently in written English may well prove of crucial importance. Though many teachers, even teachers of English, resort whenever they can to objective tests, they have not all completely abandoned the "essay" test, which requires writing. Indeed, many of the tests your child will face in a variety of situations may depend almost completely on his ability to organize and set down his ideas in acceptable written English.

Tests are of three basic kinds: aptitude tests, diagnostic tests, and achievement tests. *Aptitude tests* attempt to predict a child's probable success in a special situation; for example, in an advanced English class or in a college. They try to measure what he is capable of doing in the future, not what he has done in the past or is presently doing. In English, they aim chiefly at a child's potential ability to deal with the complexities of words, to read and listen with comprehension and perception, and to express himself with some style in writing. Theoretically, there is no way to prepare a student for an aptitude test, but in fact the more experience and training he has had in language and composition, the better he is likely to do with the test. Because of the technicalities involved in constructing a reliable measure of aptitude, most schools and colleges rely on nationally standardized aptitude tests rather than attempt to construct their own.

The aim of a *diagnostic test* is to uncover specific weaknesses in the child's skill or serious deficiencies in his knowledge. In English, such tests are used in connection with every kind of activity—spelling, dictionary use, literary knowledge, writing. Sometimes referred to as "pretests," they help the teacher by revealing where the main emphasis in his teaching should fall. The scores achieved, whether good or bad, do not (or should not) become a part of the student's achievement record, though they may later be compared with his achievement test scores to find out how successful he has been in overcoming his weaknesses. Unlike aptitude tests, diagnostic tests are more likely to be written by the teacher for his own classes, though standardized tests are available.

The most common test that children face throughout their school careers is the *achievement test,* which aims at measuring how much and how well they have learned. Every skill or bit of information covered in the English program is susceptible to achievement testing, though many authorities have serious reservations about the ability of a test to measure matters of appreciation. Achievement tests are an important part of a child's school record. They sometimes are the sole basis for deciding that a child has "passed" or "failed" a particular course or area of study. They range in importance from the daily "check-up" quiz, designed to find out how thoroughly the student has done his homework, to gigantic nationwide tests such as those of the College Entrance Examination Board and the National Merit Scholarship Program. In other words, they may be written by the individual classroom teacher, or they may be constructed by committees of nationally famous experts. At whatever level, they have one thing in common—they attempt to discover, not what the child *can* learn or what he *needs* to learn, but what he actually *has* learned from his studies.

TESTS OF WRITING

To understand what your child will encounter in the way of tests concerned with writing, here are descriptions of a few that are typical:

Having taught the uses of the comma in addresses and dates one day, the teacher gives a short quiz the following day to see how well the student has learned (remembered) to use the conventions. The test may consist of five items that he is to punctuate correctly. (*Achievement*)

At the beginning of the year, the teacher gives a test on the recognition of sentence fragments. The test consists of ten items, some of which are grammatically incomplete. The student is asked to identify and rewrite correctly those that are incomplete. On the basis of this information, the teacher decides how much time he must spend with the class as a whole on sentence fragments and which students are likely to need individual attention. (*Diagnostic*)

In his junior year of high school, the student who is applying for entrance to college may have to take the Preliminary Scholastic Aptitude Test of the College Entrance Examination Board. The test, which takes two hours, may be in several sections, alternating English and mathematics. One of its principal purposes is to measure verbal aptitude. The student is asked to give synonyms for some words; antonyms for others. He may be asked to complete word analogies. And he is asked searching questions about passages that he is given to read. The purpose of the test is to supply evidence of his ability to handle language well enough to succeed in the more difficult work of the college. The score he achieves will become part of the evidence on which his acceptance or rejection by the college will be determined. (*Aptitude*)

On the New York State Regents Comprehensive Examination in English, thirty credits of the child's score is based upon a composition written on a topic chosen from a list of about ten. The amount of credit he receives is determined by comparing his composition with a number of "models." He can afford to use about one hour of test time for writing the composition. According to the policy of the school he attends, his graduation may depend upon his achieving a "passing" score in the test. (*Achievement*)

A subsidiary effect of external examinations such as the Regents is their supervisory impact upon the schools. When tests are widely used, when back copies are available, and when the pressure for "passing" scores is high, their impact upon the school program can be widespread. Although meant as measures of achievement, they sometimes become the basis for curriculum design. Aside from cram courses built around copies of the examination from previous years, schools or individual teachers may shape the approach and the content of entire courses to prepare students for the kind of questions and approaches to subject matter reflected in these examinations.

When he enters junior high school, the child may be given a nationally standardized test, obtained from a commercial publisher. The test may have sections dealing with spelling, punctuation, sentences, usage, paragraphing, and so forth. On the basis of his score, the child may be placed in Section 1 or Section 10 in English. If the school is well run, teacher judgment or subsequent testing may determine that he should be moved from Section 10 to Section 3, or from Section 1 to Section 5. If the school is inflexible in this regard, he may well be labeled for life. (*Diagnostic*)

At the university level, the doctoral candidate is required to present a thesis. Thousands of dollars and years of effort may be at stake. A committee of distinguished professors reads and evaluates the thesis. On the basis of his command of English, as well as of his knowledge of the subject, the student may or may not receive his doctoral degree. (*Achievement*)

These are only a few of the test situations involving skill in composition that a student faces during his school years. But they certainly indicate the importance of his mastering, at the earliest possible opportunity, facility in handling the written language. Important as tests are in measuring, selecting, placing, and rewarding students, however, it must be noted that they are not all infallible. Just as there are essentially incompetent students whose photographic minds enable them to achieve undeservedly high scores, there are also capable students to whom tests are completely uncongenial. And there are tests in use whose validity and reliability are suspect. The school or parent who overlooks these possibilities runs a double risk of penalizing both gifted and weak students.

Tests that involve writing are not, of course, limited to English courses. Any subject matter teacher may use an "essay" test or may include at least an essay question or two in an otherwise "objective" test, though this is more likely to happen in the social studies than in the mathematics and sciences. Unfortunately, many of these teachers are so concerned with the "information" the child does or does not give that they tend to overlook poor writing. If the child is not penalized in some way for his slovenly composition, there is not much reason why he should try to write better. Yet at the monthly faculty meeting some of these teachers are likely to be the severest critics of the English department's efforts.

There is really no such thing as a sometime "good writer." A child should be expected at all times to express himself in the best written English of which he is capable, whether he is writing a biology report, a history test, or a thank-you note to Aunt Emma. Such situations are beyond the control of the English teacher. They are, or should be, the common concern of all other teachers or parents. One does not become a competent writer by practicing illiteracy. And this applies also to the way a student writes his tests—in a very practical way, because there *are* some teachers who do take this factor of good writing into consideration.

SOME SPECIAL TESTS OF WRITING

In the best educational sense, each word that a child writes is a test of his writing ability. Naturally, every parent would like his child to emulate a Winston Churchill, a John F. Kennedy, a William Faulkner, or even a Shakespeare. Few of our children, however, will. We are happy if they turn out to be literate. We are overjoyed if the colleges of their choice accept them. We feel twice blessed if they manage to stay in and graduate from college. But between kindergarten and college graduation lie a number of hurdles in the form of tests, that require normal competence, at least, in writing. Here are a few of the more significant.

College Entrance Tests

The growing trend among young people in recent years, not only to complete high school, but to seek some kind of higher education as well, has literally forced the colleges to set up a variety of admissions hurdles. One of these is, of course, the qualifying or entrance examination. Some of these are made up and administered by the individual college to only its own candidates for admission. Others are administered for the college by outside testing agencies.

Perhaps the most venerable of these are those tests of the College Entrance Examination Board, with headquarters at Princeton, New Jersey, and Berkeley, California. Established originally in 1900 primarily by a small group of the so-called "Ivy" colleges in the East, the Board is now composed of over 500 colleges in all parts of the country, more than 200 secondary schools, and almost 50 educational associations. Unable to cope with the recent flood tide of college applicants, the Board in 1948, with support from the Carnegie Corporation and the American Council on Education, established an independent, nonprofit organization called the Educational Testing Service, whose main functions are to carry on research in testing and to produce tests for the College Entrance Examination Board, as well as for governmental and other scholarship agencies.

A candidate for admission to any one of the member colleges of CEEB will almost certainly be asked to take the Scholastic Aptitude Test (SAT), which is a test of verbal and mathematical aptitudes. In addition, he may also be required to take the English Composition Achievement Test (ACH), which is an attempt to measure objectively his "knowledge of" writing. Not content with just an objective measure, some colleges also ask candidates to take the Writing

Sample, which is pure composition. The Sample is not graded by the testing agency but is forwarded directly to the college of the candidate's choice to make what use the Admissions Office will.

Parents brought up on the idea of an absolute 0 to 100 per cent perfect scale sometimes find it difficult to understand the percentile method used in grading tests of this kind. Students do not "pass" or "fail" these tests in the usual sense. On the basis of his responses to several hundred objective questions on the SAT (or to a fewer number of semiobjective questions on the English Composition Achievement Test), the candidate is placed on a percentile scale, ranging from 200 to 900. By this means, he is measured not against a meaningless absolute scale but against the results of all other students who try the *same* test. By the law of averages, most students find their positions in the 400 to 600 percentile range. On the basis of its experience and number of openings, each college then decides its own cutoff point in judging applicants. This score is only one part of the admissions picture, however, and a college as highly selective as Harvard may accept an applicant whose test score falls below the usual cutoff point—if his record gives evidence of other significant qualities.

For many years after its inception, the College Board asked all candidates to write compositions, which were read and evaluated by committees of teachers and professors appointed by the Board. When the number of college applicants in the 1930s and 1940s rose so sharply that the Board was no longer able to read "with justice" the overwhelming number of compositions written, an objective test of composition skills was substituted. During the war years of the 1940s, this test went largely unchallenged, but as our military concerns lessened and we began to take stock of our cultural and educational achievements, it became a center of controversy.

Critics attacked the test on two points: first, they challenged the ability of an objective test "about writing" to measure a person's actual ability "to write." Second, they maintained that the objective test encouraged teachers to put more emphasis on knowledge of how compositions should be written than upon the essential practice of writing. In its defense, the College Board cited studies to show that objective tests are fairly reliable predictors of college success, more so than written compositions, because no one has yet devised (or probably ever will do so) a commonly agreed upon method for evaluating the writing of an individual. Several "experts" reading a given composition inevitably assign it a variety of scores. Nevertheless, in response to the popular criticism, the Board in 1960 began to offer the Writing Sample for the use of those colleges that desired it. At the time of this writing, the Board is engaged in an extensive reevaluation of its entire English testing offering—an indication that they themselves are not completely satisfied with their present testing program.

Selection Tests for Scholarships

Although no state or national scholarship test is based solely on a candidate's writing ability, some do give it a major emphasis. An important section of the New York State Scholarship Examination, for example, consists of a so-called "qualifying composition test." After the objective parts of the test are graded, the compositions of the successful candidates are read. No matter how high the objective scores, candidates who do not demonstrate a desirable level of writing ability cannot hope to receive a state scholarship.

Other important examinations, like those of the National Merit Scholarship program, require no actual writing but do have sections dealing with verbal and compositional skills.

NCTE Achievement Awards Program

The only nationally important test program that deals primarily with writing skill is that instituted by the National Council of Teachers of English in 1958. The basis for these awards is no single test, but a variety of items. Each candidate submits an autobiography of 250 to 300 words, a sample of his writing representing his best work, and an impromptu composition written in no more than one hour on a subject chosen by NCTE. In addition the candidate is given (under supervision) a standardized test on usage and writing skill and on literary awareness.

The total number of awards in each state is limited to the number of Congressional representatives of that state. The number of candidates which a high school may nominate depends upon the school's enrollment in grades 10 to 12; with up to 500 students, for example, a school may enter one eleventh-grade candidate; between 500 and 999, two candidates, and so on. The brochure listing all finalists is sent to all college admissions officers, college English department chairmen, governors, and members of Congress. In the few years of its existence, the program has been responsible for the granting of large sums of scholarship money to students whose exceptional English ability might otherwise have gone unnoted.

WRITING FOR TESTS

Writing for tests is no different from writing for other purposes except that it is done under greater pressure. Instead of several days or an evening in which to collect ideas, organize them, write them out, and revise them, the child may have no more than an hour or two, perhaps only twenty minutes (as on one important national test), in which to carry out this complex process. In addition, he is under the added nervous tension that a test situation inevitably produces.

Perhaps more than anything else, it is the tension involved in a test situation that causes otherwise well-prepared students to write badly. Granted that some students suffer tension only because they have not done the required work, the fact should be recognized that others do poorly because they are by nature "slow" writers. And the word "slow" here does not mean "retarded," but rather that some people need time to mull over their ideas, to organize, and to find the right words for them. Even professional writers vary in this respect. Some can turn out several thousand words a day over a long period; others, by their own admission, consider they have done well to turn out a single sentence in that time.

Your interest, naturally, is how to help *your* child to write better both in general and on these tests. The only answer we can give to that question is that no one writes well on a test who doesn't know how to write well in other situations. For most people, learning to write well is a lengthy, often painful, process. Hiring a tutor at the zero hour is not likely to have much effect upon your child's test results. He will begin to learn to write well when he wants to learn to write well. But "wanting to" is only the starting point. "Writing well," for most of us, is the product of much practice. One does not become a good writer any more quickly than one becomes a good tennis player, actor, cook, or automobile mechanic.

Perhaps the most helpful thing you, as a parent, can do to help your child is, in your own mind, to put tests in their proper perspective. They are important and they are inevitable. But in the long run, there are worse things in this life than failing a school test, however disastrous the immediate results appear to be.

10

No other subject offered by the school covers so much ground and is so difficult to define as the study of English. Add to this the infinite variety of ways in which a teacher may approach the subject (influenced as he is by such matters as training, personality, background, likes and dislikes, local school and community demands), and one begins to realize why "English programs" in different parts of the country or even in adjoining communities may be so unlike. As a matter of fact, two English teachers in adjacent rooms teaching the same material may use such different methods that a visitor would find it difficult to believe that he was watching in both classes a lesson prescribed by the school's English syllabus. Also, he might find it difficult to judge which of the two teachers is doing the more effective job.

In spite of the difficulties presented by such human considerations, most schools do attempt to set down the English program they would like to have their teachers follow. In large communities, this program may be decided upon by a committee of teachers and supervisors representing all schools. Their findings are generally written down formally, published as a syllabus or course of study, and given to each teacher as a guide. In smaller communities or in single schools, courses of study may take the less impressive form of mimeographed sheets, or consist simply of verbal agreements arrived at in faculty lounge discussions (or in the boiler room, if no provision is made for faculty conference—which is often the case).

In the main, English courses of study tend to be conservative, reflecting the skills and materials that the student will be tested on, the textbooks in use, the vocational opportunities in the community, the recommendations of authorities, and sources of help such as the National Council of Teachers of English and other professional organizations.

Distressingly few courses of study in English show a disposition to experiment with recent (though not untested) materials and methods of presentation. This is only partly understandable, for only through experimentation and capitalization on new ideas and methods can we hope to move ahead in teaching the young more effectively.

Actually, the school with a staff adventurous and energetic enough to accept the extra effort that new programs entail will come out ahead in most cases, no matter how successful or unsuccessful the "idea" itself proves to be. Because they are traveling a new road, the staff is alert and enthusiastic in a way that teachers following the old, familiar—and often tired—routine can never be. This enthusiasm communicates itself to children who, in turn, become excited about and involved in the subject in a way that normally they would not. (In psychology research, this is known as the "halo" or Hawthorne effect.) It is rather surprising, in view of this well-authenticated phenomenon, that more schools do not try new methods of teaching —and that parents so relentlessly fight such efforts when teachers do have the imagination and energy to try "something new." If such a condition prevailed in medicine, of course, we would not today be profiting from such discoveries as penicillin and the many other life-saving "wonder drugs."

What kind of school does experiment, especially with the teaching of English? One's first guess might be the fairly well-to-do suburban community, which has a better-trained and better-paid staff and unusual resources—a Bronxville, a Newton, or a New Trier, for example. But this no longer is generally the case. The school today that employs new methods is more likely to be the one that has reached a frustration point, where anything seems preferable to that which obviously has not succeeded, or it is the school fortunate enough to have within its staff a core of individuals who will not accept the cautious philosophy that the old way is the safe and therefore superior way of proceeding. More often than not, such schools have the poorest equipment and most meager student back-ground. They may even be city schools in disadvantaged neighbor-hoods that have been freed from the demands of the general syllabus.

Though some schools may experiment with new content, as in the schools that are trying "structural" in place of traditional grammar, most experimental programs are more likely to concentrate on new methods of organizing and teaching the old content. In some schools the change is no more than that of applying methods that are new to the local situation but have been tried widely in schools elsewhere. In others, it is the introduction of completely new techniques, such as team teaching and lay readers, for example. In other words, the experimentation may be so limited and conservative that the com-munity is unaware it is happening, or it may be so radical that it calls for complete reorganization of the school's program—usually ac-companied by community-wide repercussions.

The following are brief descriptions of some of the programs that schools in various parts of the country have set up in an effort to improve the teaching of composition (in most cases, as part of the whole subject of English). They are of both types, conservative and radical. No attempt is made here to judge the strengths or weaknesses of these programs. Perhaps the school your child attends is already trying all or parts of these plans; perhaps it has even introduced methods not mentioned here. (More power to it—it deserves your intelligent support!)

ENGLISH AND COMPOSITION IN A NONGRADED SCHOOL

One of the more radical and exciting experiments in education is the nongraded school, and one of the most publicized of these is the Melbourne High School, twenty-five miles from Cape Kennedy, Florida. An influx of children of skilled technicians in a traditionally conventional rural school system forced authorities to search for a new kind of school organization in which all levels of intellectual ability might find a challenge. The result is a program that has discarded grade-level, age-level measures. Instead, at Melbourne, a student can move ahead as fast as he can master the prescribed material.

Students entering the high school are "sorted" on the basis of nationally standardized achievement tests and assigned to "phases" rather than to grades.

Phase 1. Subjects are concerned largely with "remedial" work.
Phase 2. Subjects deal with "basic" skills.
Phase 3. Subjects are designed for students seeking an "average" education.
Phase 4. Subjects are provided for students desiring education in "considerable" depth.
Phase 5. Subjects are open only to students willing to assume responsibility for their own learning and to go beyond the boundaries of a single course in their study.
Phase 6. This "Quest" phase is intended for students with well-developed creative talents who wish to research a special area, either to develop creative powers or in quest of knowledge. A student may spend from one to three hours a day in Quest.
Phase X. Nonacademic subjects like typing and physical education are ungraded but also unphased.

A student entering Melbourne High who is weak in English (presumably including composition) enters Phase 1. He devotes two hours a day instead of the usual one hour to the subject until he has raised himself to the standard set by the school. If his particular weakness is writing, for example, he spends this time in a writing laboratory, containing a maximum of fifteen students. Descriptions of the program, unfortunately, deal more fully with the handling of reading and literature than of composition. Presumably, composition in Phase 5 is a part of the research process and is closely integrated with the student's special interest.

The program is noteworthy for its insistence upon the importance of the individual, upon the ideal of "excellence," and upon the superiority of "inquiry" to memorization of facts as the basic and most rewarding educational activity.

AN ENGLISH COMPOSITION LABORATORY

To raise the writing level of its students, the Greensboro, North Carolina, High School has introduced a laboratory plan. The details of this plan were worked out by the local staff in consultation with Arno Jewett, Director of the National Education Association—Dean Langmuir Project on Improving English Composition.

This plan attempts to strengthen the emphasis upon composition by using lay readers of student composition, double periods for those who need it, and closer integration of composition writing with other subject fields.

In this program, each laboratory teacher has two classes with double periods, each set up in combination with a non-English teacher. An eighth-grader, for example, has a double period of English and social studies; a ninth-grader, of English and science; a tenth-grader, of English and American history, and so on. In every case, the teachers work and plan together.

Compositions are graded both by a lay reader and by the subject matter teacher, and each composition receives two grades—one for writing technique and one for content:

B. Science teacher's grade for content.
C. Lay reader's grade for writing performance, or English teacher's evaluation.

From the description, one assumes that the English teacher is mainly responsible for instructing in technique, as well as for reading student papers.

In general, this program appears to put chief emphasis on technique, which seems to mean conventional grammar, spelling, punctuation, and on content derived largely from the other subject matter fields.

A GRADE 1 TO 12 INTEGRATED COMPOSITION PROGRAM

A description in summary of the complete program in composition of the San Diego City Schools reveals careful integration of writing activities with speech and literature, and an effort to maintain a balance between "creative" and expositional writing. This program also uses lay readers at the secondary level.

In the elementary school, written language is viewed as an extension of oral language. The program begins with the teacher writing as children dictate their own individual messages or sentences for a composite story. As soon as a child acquires the necessary handwriting skill, he begins to write his own "story" with the teacher helping him with formation of letters, spacing, and spelling until he is ready to work independently in the writer's corner with self-help aids.

In the primary grades "practical" writing begins with such experiences as children writing their names, adding a caption to art work, or labeling a rack for a collection. This is followed by simple announcements, records of events and weather, and directions or explanations such as how to plant seeds or bulbs. Letter writing is also an important activity beginning in the first grade.

"Creative" writing is encouraged from the very beginning of the program as groups work on composite stories. A three-day sequence is frequently used for a primary class writing project. On the first day the teacher might read a story or show a filmstrip. Interesting action and picture words are recorded on the chalkboard as children discuss the story. On the second day the words are reviewed and the discussion continued as the teacher introduces a picture related to the subject of the story or filmstrip. While they discuss the picture, the children think about what they might write in their stories. Time is given for the children to write, and their stories are collected by the teacher. Before the third day, the teacher reviews the stories and plans a period in which children proofread and evaluate their writing and are given an opportunity to revise their stories.

In the upper elementary grades, letter-writing instruction is continued. Here the aim is to stimulate a flow of "natural" instilled writing, emphasizing content first and then form. Other kinds of practical expository writing are also encouraged such as preparing an explanation for a science display. Notetaking and outlining are two skills included in the curriculum, and proofreading by the student of his own work is emphasized as a part of the program in teaching usage and mechanics of writing.

In the personal writing program for older elementary school children, an attempt is made to establish a classroom atmosphere conducive to releasing creative abilities. The teacher takes time to note novel, fresh, or unusual incidents. He also tries to build a feeling for rhythm in language, encouraging natural expression as much as possible. Frequent opportunities to write are provided. The district publishes an annual creative writing booklet containing the work of elementary school children.

In the secondary school, composition is an integral part of a total language arts program. Ideas are introduced into the classroom through literature, expanded and clarified through class analysis and discussion, and finally synthesized and refined through writing experiences. Both practical and creative types of writing are included in the program, the emphasis varying with the ability level of the student. Lay readers are employed to increase the amount of writing that can be evaluated by an adult. The goals of the program include the development of writing skills that are fundamental to good communication, and the stimulation of intellectual curiosity and critical thinking.

THE LANGUAGE-EXPERIENCE APPROACH OF
SAN DIEGO COUNTY SCHOOLS

Chapters 1 and 2 referred to the widely recognized language-experience program, which is being experimentally compared with "traditional," more prevalent ways of teaching the English language arts. Children using the language-experience approach start their writing activities early in first grade, with the teacher acting as secretary to individuals and groups who talk about their current interests and intriguing experience. The children are learning to use manuscript writing at the same time and are soon able to copy part or all of what the teacher has written down. They also start individual files of words that are used so that such words can be spelled correctly as soon as independent writing begins.

From the beginning, these pupil-dictated sentences and stories are the basis for reading lessons. In effect, then, children in the language-experience program write before they read. Actually, all the English language arts move along together as children speak and listen, write and read as part of one comprehensive learning activity, which soon includes easily read trade books.

Whenever individual stories are dictated to the teacher, the children not occupied in such dictation are drawing or painting large illustrations, which will accompany the story that has been or soon will be dictated. Similar illustrative activities accompany independent writing at later stages. The four compositions that follow were written as children were learning to use cursive handwriting instead of the earlier manuscript-letter forms. The first composition is a factual report by a boy who knew much about lizards, so common in his area.

> The lizard is a very fast creature. He lives in the Mojave Desert. He is white and black and many other colors too. The lizard has a fat body and a very little tail.

A child in Brier Patch School, La Mesa-Spring Valley School District, contributed to a class booklet labeled *My Pencil Is a Sailing Ship* as follows:

> My school is a harbor full of gentle boats. Every classroom is a yacht club and the playground is the sea. All the boats are trying to catch me.[1]

Two other children in the same school were full of imaginative questions, which they wrote in verse form for the same booklet.

> Where is Fairy Land?
> Over the meadow?
> Or in the stream?
> In the moonlight?
> Or in a dream?
> In a hole?
> Or in the wall?
> Or maybe
> Any place at all![2]

One girl, while not inclined to rhyme, made her vivid contribution to the Brier Patch's booklet, No. 3.

> A summer night brings moonlight down by the valley. and shows its splendor over the lakes, hills and seas. The trees rustle their leaves as a plane goes by. As I lie in my bed and look out my window, I hear people walk by and their shadows shine merrily.[3]

[1] From *My Pencil Is a Sailing Ship*, a publication of the Brier Patch School in the La Mesa-Spring Valley School District, La Mesa, California. Used by permission of the District, David D. Pascoe, assistant superintendent, instruction, and Nancy L. Leeds, Teacher-Enrichment Curriculum Department.

[2] *Ibid.*

[3] From *All Aboard for Poetry Land,* Volume III, a publication of the Brier Patch School in the La Mesa-Spring Valley School District, La Mesa, California. Used by permission of the District, David D. Pascoe, assistant superintendent, instruction, and Nancy L. Leeds, Teacher-Enrichment Curriculum Department.

SMALLER CLASSES AND LIGHTER LOAD FOR
ENGLISH TEACHERS

One program that has taken seriously the recommendations of James B. Conant, the National Council of Teachers of English, and other professionally concerned groups—that if the quality of student writing is to be improved, the number of students assigned a teacher daily must achieve a more realistic level—is that of the Pittsburgh Public Schools.

> The reduction of each English teacher's assignment to four classes, totaling no more than 100 pupils, with a "theme" period in addition to a regular preparation period, soon brought positive results. Frequent departmental meetings, conferences, demonstrations, comparisons of compositions, numerous sheets of mimeographed materials, and the use of audiovisual aids have produced an English departmental solidarity and a continuity of teaching and learning processes that are producing both teacher and pupil improvement in writing.[4]

Westinghouse High School, which enrolls 2,600 students, began its new English program in 1958. As part of its plan, 100 of the most able students are arbitrarily assigned to special classes. Teacher committees work out units and lists of suggested activities for the whole group.

> A course in grammar accompanied the assignments, not as an isolated body of instruction, but as an instrument guide for writing, the various tools for which are utilized in each theme problem. This integration of grammar with composition constitutes, perhaps, a unique contribution of the program to the general methodology of instruction in English.[5]

Because the reduction in English teacher loads to 100 students daily makes it practicable, this plan places a major emphasis upon theme-a-week writing. Nine English teachers were added to the staff to make this possible. English teachers meet during their theme-reading periods in a common room to grade and discuss student compositions.

Westinghouse High School is the second largest high school in Pittsburgh, and it has a high percentage of Negro students. A similar

---

[4] "The Principal's Point of View," *The English Program at Westinghouse High School,* Pittsburgh Schools, **XXXVI** (January, April 1962), p. 153. Reprinted by permission of Pittsburgh Public Schools.

[5] "Background and Organization," *The English Program at Westinghouse High School, ibid.*

program was instituted in 1962 in Peabody High School, the secondary high school with the second highest percentage of college-bound students in the city.

A TEACHER-WRITTEN HANDBOOK FOR WRITTEN COMPOSITION

Members of the Houston Public Schools' Writing Standards Committee met from 1961 to 1963 in a number of after-school sessions and worked individually and in small groups to develop a handbook for written composition for the use of teachers from grades 7 to 12.

The handbook presents sequential steps for teaching expository writing, descriptive writing, narrative writing, writing of social letters, and the writing of business letters. Each section contains samples of desirable student writing. It is offered to the teachers, however, not as a prescribed syllabus, but as a source of ideas and information, with the suggestion that teachers adapt or draw from the materials provided in whatever way seems most advantageous to a particular class or individual.

The hope of the Writing Standards Committee is that the material will be considered a model insofar such practices as the following are concerned:

Vigorous, well-organized teaching of written composition.

Teaching of basic principles by the inductive method.

Thorough teaching of principles before theme writing is begun.

Use of the class period for the actual writing.

Active supervision of the writing as it is done in class.

Student evaluation of one another's papers, according to established criteria.

Proofreading by the student of his own writing.

Correlation of the teaching of sentence structure and usage with the teaching of written composition.

Basic to the program presented in the handbook are the beliefs that specific attention to organization and detail will result in improved writing and that this emphasis will not interfere with a child's creativity. Further, it subscribes to the thesis that types of sentence structure are best acquired by the student when "emphasized and used in specific assignments according to a definite plan."

COMPOSITION IN A SCHOOL FOR THE GIFTED

Hunter College High School is a public high school for gifted girls who are drawn from all of the public, private, and parochial schools of New York City. The median IQ of its 1,150 students, grades 7 to 12, is between 145 and 150, and more than 98 per cent of the girls enter college.

The unique feature of the writing program, which places a heavy emphasis upon both creative and closely analytic writing, is that there is no formal program. One of the chief qualifications for hiring staff members is evidence that they have had exceptional experience with written English. Each teacher is then given complete freedom to approach the teaching of composition (and all other aspects of English) according to his particular talents and philosophy. Almost all of the expository writing grows out of the reading and discussion of literature. The rationale for this "nonprogram" is the belief that good writing is possible only where there is sound thinking, and that sound thinking develops not from a planned series of steps, but from the day-to-day use of the mind in dealing with the important ideas, experiences, and values presented in good literature.

Concurrent with classroom practice in composition, the English department as a whole carries on a continuing campaign to encourage self-initiated writing. Each year, for example, a schoolwide "Writers' Workshop" is organized. During the week of the workshop, teachers of all courses are invited to carry on writing projects of a creative nature related to their subject. During this week, too, authors, editors, journalists, and advertising writers are invited to come to the school to discuss informally with small groups of students the techniques they use and the problems they face as writers. The stimulus of such opportunities leads to a heavy outpouring of independent writing.

Such a program is probably possible only with students who are highly verbal by nature and are strongly motivated to develop their exceptional talents. Such students, it is assumed, need to be given every opportunity to accept personal responsibility for developing clarity and style.

A careful observer may have noticed that there is a good deal of overlapping among these various programs. Even the most unusual shares some common characteristics with the more conventional. English *is* English, after all, no matter how it is taught. At the same time, a fair-minded observer can hardly help concluding that there is more than one way to approach this complex problem—helping the young to express themselves more effectively in the difficult medium of written English. For this very reason, parents should try to be sympathetic with and not blindly critical of their school if its English staff makes an effort to improve its teaching of composition—even when the effort appears, on the surface at least, unorthodox.

11

This book has discussed the more important aspects of the teaching of composition in the schools today. Along the way, it has also tried to drop hints of ways in which you, as a parent, can help your children in their efforts to acquire skill in this essential communication process. Now in summary, perhaps a list of the specific steps that you can take to help your son or daughter to become a better writer is in order.

Many of you are probably only too willing to admit that you had too little composition training yourself in school to be able to help your children in any direct way now. Even those of you who did have (or have learned it the hard way, since) find that your children are not especially receptive to your suggestions and advice, especially after they have reached the age of ten or eleven. The teacher of English, whether at the elementary or the secondary level, is usually better able than you to handle the technical problems of teaching composition—though it must be admitted that a good many teachers are not as well trained for this particular responsibility as they should be. Still, if the child has any disposition or ability to learn, the teacher is, psychologically at least, in a better position to motivate and guide the development of writing skill.

But no matter how effective the teacher may be, the parent cannot escape completely all reponsibility, nor does the wise parent want to. Here then are some of the ways in which you, assuming you are of the latter group, can be of real help, primarily to your children but also to the school in its efforts to teach them to become more competent writers.

1. *Encourage your child to verbalize—to express his ideas both in speech and writing—beginning at the earliest possible age.* The old admonition that "a child should be seen and not heard" may have produced more peaceful families in the old days (though this has never been proved), but it certainly must have robbed countless generations of children of invaluable experience with the use of language. Acknowledging that there are other factors to be considered, normally

the family in which the child is encouraged to "speak his piece" is likely to be happier and, in the long run, to produce the more effective and literate adults. We do not refer here, of course, to meaningless babbling or to rude interruption, but to the verbalization of ideas that are important to the child, his family, and indirectly to the culture. In this connection, you perhaps should note that discriminating between the "meaningless" and the "meaningful" in child talk is not always easy. The parent should beware of judging the ideas of the six- or the sixteen-year-old by standards of thirty-six or even twenty-six-year-olds. Time and maturity have a way of making the world look different!

2. *Be a sympathetic, but not an interfering, audience to your child.* Whenever a child (or an adult, for that matter) speaks or writes, he likes to think that someone is listening to or reading his words. Although the family should not be a child's sole audience, it should, especially for younger children, be an important and understanding audience. Nothing is probably more frustrating to well-intentioned parents than a child who will not communicate. Sometimes this is due to conditions that have no connection whatsoever with language. But it should never result from a child's feeling that his ideas are unwelcome, that his English is "bad," or that his speech and writing are an utter disappointment to his parents.

3. *Create in your child an interest in words.* At every opportunity call attention to words that are especially well used or that are particularly interesting for other reasons. Words of this kind appear constantly in ordinary conversation ("Why does Aunt Emily say to-may-to, but we all say to-mah-to?"), on TV and radio commercials and programs ("Why do things taste good *like* they should?"), and in newspapers and books. When a child becomes curious about words as such, his vocabulary will grow many times its normal rate.

Educational word games such as Scrabble and anagrams may help too, and older children will be intrigued by the crossword puzzle. Incidentally, the parent who has himself never paid much attention to "words" may reap an unexpected bonus from these activities! One is never too old to learn.

4. *From the time he begins to talk, teach your child to observe and report accurately the world around him.* No other skill may be more important to him through all of his life than this. Yet do not forget that not all children are equally endowed. In his efforts to verbalize his world, a child may be handicapped by poor hearing, poor vision, color blindness, tone deafness, or any one of a number of other sense deficiencies. In one way or another, nature usually

compensates for such deficiencies, but in any case a child should neither be expected to perform the impossible nor should he usually be "babied" because of his deficiencies. Unless the problem is clearly organic, he can and should be expected to improve, though one child may not develop as far or as fast as another. Never, above all else, compare the performance of one of your children to another's.

5. *Encourage your child to read good writing.* Next to direct experience, the reading a child does is usually his most important source of new words and ideas. Furthermore, because language learning is mainly an imitative process, exposure to the sentence patterns and paragraphing of a good writer is bound to influence the child's own writing. But "good" writing does not mean only the "classics." Familiarity with the writing of other ages—of Chaucer, Shakespeare, Swift, and others—cannot help enriching a person's use of language, but good contemporary writing is also important. The student, after all, must speak and write the English of his own time.

6. *Provide your child with a variety of experiences.* Though first-hand experience is generally the more stimulating, when this is not available, the vicarious experience offered by motion pictures and television (in moderation) should not be scorned. Not every family can afford extensive travel or tickets to important plays and operas, but if they put their minds to it, most families today can provide their children with an enriching variety of experiences. Libraries, museums, state and national parks, concerts, and summer theaters —every section of the country has cultural advantages of one kind or another to offer. Such experiences broaden the individual's perspectives, if he has been alerted, and are an important factor in the growth of his vocabulary.

7. *Insist on "real" letter writing, and set a good example yourself.* One of the commonest and most important writing activities that adults engage in is letter writing, both social and business. Though schools spend considerable time on the forms of letters, they find it difficult to set up practice letter-writing assignments that have real meaning for the student. Yet most homes and families offer many opportunities for children to write friendly letters, invitations, thank-you notes, business letters of order and complaint—letters that go to living people and have a genuine purpose. Far too many adults put off or neglect entirely this important avenue of communication, largely because the habit of letter writing was not implanted in their school experience and not encouraged at home.

8. *See that such basic writing tools are always on hand as paper, pencil, pen, or typewriter, a writing desk or surface, and a reliable,*

up-to-date dictionary. Most important, of course, is having a place available in the home where your child can write (or complete his other studies) undisturbed by family activities, television, and assorted other distractions. Such a place should be well supplied with paper suitable for both rough and final drafts, and with writing implements. Typing is not required in most schools and colleges, but a child who can use a typewriter has certain advantages over his nontyping class-mates, even if he practices only the "hunt and peck" system. Not only do neatly typed papers put the reader in a more receptive frame of mind, but the writer himself is better able to judge his work if it is in the form of print rather than in the longhand that is often difficult for even the one who wrote it to decipher.

Special note must be taken here of the importance of a reliable, up-to-date dictionary. No book is more generally useful to the edu-cated person at every age than the dictionary. For a writer it is indispensable, and its use must be made habitual, starting in child-hood. Yet many homes have no dictionary at all, or at best have only a ragged "antique" or a "supermarket special" dictionary for the family to use.

Any dictionary is of course better than none. But today there are good dictionaries for every age and purpose easily available. There are dictionaries for the elementary, for the intermediate, for the high school, and for the college student. There are even inexpensive paper-back editions of some good dictionaries. Unabridged dictionaries are the most complete of all; however, they are not ordinarily the most usable kinds, nor do most modern homes have space in which to store them. For most purposes (for meaning, pronunciation, spelling, and word division), a good high school or collegiate level dictionary is of most use to children at the secondary level.

9. *Don't do your child's writing or revising for him.* It would be ridiculous to think that normally concerned parents never give help to their children when they can. This help may or may not be neces-sary, but if given, it should at least be offered inductively. If you want to be helpful, don't tell your child to "put in a comma here" or "capitalize that word." Instead, be *inductive.* Ask questions that will force your child to think out his problems for himself. "Should there be some kind of punctuation here?" or "Is that the right spelling?" You may advisedly work closely with your first- or second-grade child and give considerable help in planning and in spelling, but remember that a child who always has a parental crutch to rely on will be a long time in accepting responsibility for his own writing, even as an adult.

10. *Be an example to your child—be honest: in writing, discourage plagiarism, however innocent.* Even more reprehensible than doing your child's writing for him is encouraging him to pass off other people's writing as his own. Before the law, this practice is considered a crime equal to that of taking another person's money or property. Each year the sponsors of both local and nationally significant writing contests are plagued by dishonest entries. Because no one person has read everything that has been written, these plagiarisms are sometimes hard for judges to detect. In one unfortunate case, a boy placed first in a national fiction contest. To the chagrin of the judges and the disgrace to the boy, his teacher, and his school, half a year later a dentist from the opposite end of the country reported to the contest sponsors that he recognized the story as one that had appeared *fifteen years before* in a little-known magazine. The case was particularly regrettable because the writer happened to be a brilliant student who was quite capable of writing a story even better than the one he chose to steal.

A teacher can explain the morality involved in the act of plagiarism and thus may keep most student writers from making innocent mistakes. But he cannot control deliberate dishonesty. A child's character, after all, is basically the responsibility of the parents.

11. *Don't ridicule or condemn the teacher in the child's presence.* In English more than in any other subject, your child's success may be affected by his confidence in the teacher. Not all teachers, admittedly, are equally able or well trained (nor are all doctors, lawyers, and automobile mechanics, for that matter!). Thus, when a child is assigned to a teacher who seems for one reason or another less effective than most, your adverse criticism at the family supper table can only weaken your child's confidence in his teacher. Certainly such behind-the-scenes quarterbacking will not help the teacher to become a better teacher, however much you may desire it. If you have a complaint, discuss it first with the teacher.

12. *Don't demand the impossible of your child: be realistic about his capabilities.* Educationally, it is as dangerous to demand too much as it is not to demand enough. If the English program is shallow and unchallenging, your child will find it dull and unrewarding. He will respond with a minimum investment of his ability. On the other hand, to set goals that are clearly impossible for him to attain is to invite disaster. Whatever the field of human endeavor, nothing succeeds like success—or at least the possibility of success. Common sense tells us not to waste time trying to accomplish the impossible; an old folk

saying, in fact, advises, "Don't bang your head against a stone wall."

Many parents, unfortunately, find it difficult or they literally refuse to assess realistically their child's capabilities. They demand that he be assigned to an advanced placement class, for example, when he is doing his very best in a regular English class. They make the child's life and their own miserable driving to get him into Ivy University when the child's inclinations, test scores, and academic performance generally indicate to the unbiased that his only chance for satisfaction and success lies in the less demanding (but for him more suitable) program of an intellectually less exacting school.

The skills of English are basic to a child's success at all grade levels, especially the skills of reading and writing. If a parent is not able to judge for himself his child's proficiency with these skills, then he certainly should be willing to share the school's (that is, the English teacher's) professional judgment in the matter. In turn, the school has its solemn responsibility to determine, as accurately as it is possible to do, the child's potentialities. One baffling and constantly recurring question to teachers is "How much and what kind of composition training is actually necessary for these children?"

13. *Be encouraging and, if possible, constructive in commenting on your child's writing.* Resist the easy temptation to point out, first of all, his spelling, punctuation, or other mechanical errors. Begin instead with a favorable comment about his ideas, remembering that they should be judged again according to the writer's age and maturity level, not according to your own. Your purpose, bear in mind, is *not* to impress on the child how much he doesn't know, nor is it to impress upon him how much more you know than he does.

Your purpose is, or should be, to add to your child's self-confidence as a writer—to encourage him to want to go on writing down his ideas for you and others to read. For many children at the elementary level, a bulletin board, hung in a moderately conspicuous place in the home, may serve to bring their composition work to the attention of the entire family. Once you have established a good writer-audience relationship with your child, then the way may be clear to make occasional suggestions about the mechanical flaws in his writing.

It is only fair to note at this point that some parents and children, for reasons that have nothing to do with writing or the study of English, may never achieve this kind of favorable relationship. In fact, where teenagers are involved, lack of communication between parent and child is possibly a more normal state of affairs than not! At least a part of this trouble may stem from the parents' failure to set up a trunk line early enough. The child who begins early in his elementary years to view his parents as an understanding and enthusiastic audience is not as likely to shut them off when he slips into adolescence.

In making these suggestions, we are fully aware that parents who achieve a 100 per cent batting average in applying them successfully must be paragons—and probably have exceptional children to begin with! All we can say at this point is that the closer you come to practicing the suggestions offered in this chapter, the more helpful you will be to your child—and to the school in which, after all, the responsibility rests for helping to make him a more competent writer. Needless to say, the corollary is also true. Your failure to take an active interest in his writing may not block your child from becoming a competent writer, but it certainly won't make the road easier for him.